SIMPLE RECIPES, GOOD FOOD

SIMPLE RECIPES, GOOD FOOD
A COOKBOOK

5-INGREDIENT | 30-MINUTE | MAKE AHEAD
ONE POT | SLOW COOKER

JESSECA HALLOWS

Photography by Linda Xiao

ROCKRIDGE
PRESS

For general information on our other products and services or to obtain technical support, please contact our Customer Care Department within the United States at (866) 744-2665, or outside the United States at (510) 253-0500.

Rockridge Press publishes its books in a variety of electronic and print formats. Some content that appears in print may not be available in electronic books, and vice versa.

Interior and Cover Designer: John Clifford
Art Producer: Samantha Ulban
Editor: Laura Apperson
Production Manager: Michael Kay
Production Editor: Melissa Edeburn
Photography © 2020 Linda Xiao. Food Styling by Brett Regot.
Author photo courtesy of Megan Weaver Photography.

ISBN: Print 978-1-64739-871-2 | eBook 978-1-64739-548-3
R0

To Donna, my amazing aunt, who is always eager
to provide amazing feedback and offer words of encouragement
when needed. I am so grateful to have her as my helper.

CONTENTS

INTRODUCTION

Quick-and-easy recipes are my bread and butter. I love creating tasty dishes with minimal ingredients that come together with practically no effort. My website, One Sweet Appetite, is based on exactly such dishes.

Years ago, when I first met my husband, I found the way to his heart was through his stomach. While trying new recipes, I realized how much I love to be in the kitchen. I experienced a major learning curve, mainly because I had never cooked anything beyond boxed mac and cheese, but over time I found myself becoming more and more confident with cooking basics. I spent hours in the kitchen whipping up different recipes. I wanted to soak up as much foodie knowledge as possible and put those skills to work.

My love for cooking grew with every new recipe, and I wanted to share my skills and experience with all beginner cooks and bakers. That is when I started a website to showcase my recipes. In every post, I like to be transparent, recounting failures along with the successes. Keeping things real, while providing essential tips, has helped me develop loyal followers with varying levels of culinary skill.

One of the most frequent requests I receive is for basic, yet delicious, recipes. Readers want go-to dishes they can reach for in a pinch—for party planning and busy weeknights and to satisfy a sweet tooth.

This book presents my favorite simple recipes. From breakfast to dessert, they will fit easily into your menu. Each includes one or more of five labels: 5-Ingredient, 30-Minute, Make Ahead, One Pot/ Pan, and Slow Cooker. Skip to the back of the book to find an index of the recipes organized by category (see page 162). You'll also see Dairy-Free, Gluten-Free, and Nut-Free labels wherever appropriate.

Beyond simple and delicious recipes, you will find multiple cooking resources, including information on kitchen staples, and tools, tips, and tricks for customizing dishes.

With this book, you will build your confidence in the kitchen, master culinary basics, and find delight in cooking.

CHAPTER 1

GET READY FOR SIMPLE, DELICIOUS MEALS

Getting dinner on the table has never been easier! *Simple Recipes, Good Food* is filled with delicious go-to recipes for any occasion.

Whether you are searching for a slow cooker dinner, one pot/pan meal, 30-minute go-to recipe, make ahead favorite, or 5-ingredient dessert, there is a delicious dish in this book just for you. So, let's get started!

ORGANIZED AND EFFICIENT SHOPPING

Browsing the grocery store aisles and discovering new products is like a treasure hunt, but the tedious task of doing this week after week can get old. I have put together some of my favorite tips to help you make your shopping experience quicker and easier.

1. **Check the ads:** Flipping through your local grocery store ads before you head to the store can be helpful. Plan your meals around what's on sale.

2. **Always shop with a list:** Planning your meals is an easy way to make sure you only make one trip to the store. Create a list of everything you'll need before you leave home and refer to it while shopping. Having a revolving list of go-to meals, like the ones in this book, makes this task simple.

3. **Buy in bulk:** Is an often-used ingredient on sale? Consider buying it in bulk. This helps cut costs and builds your food supply at the same time. Some great things to look for include canned goods and anything that can be frozen. Meats, when stored properly, can be frozen for up to four months. Produce is also a great item to consider buying in bulk. Most fresh fruit can be frozen for up to one year and fresh vegetables can last in your freezer for 18 months. Consider dicing onions or bell peppers before freezing them for an at-the-ready solution when preparing a dish.

4. **Shop the center aisles first:** Most grocery stores keep pantry items and shelf-stable goods in the center of the store, so add those to your cart first and end with dairy, meats, and cheeses. That way, the refrigerated items stay chilled longer until you transport them home.

5. **Never shop hungry:** You tend to add more to your cart when you're hungry, which increases how much you spend and, perhaps, waste. You also grab things that seem appealing at the time, but then sit in the pantry unused. When you buy without a plan, you may end up without all the ingredients you need for the week's meals, or you may forget why you thought an impulse buy seemed appealing in the first place.

HELPFUL COOKING HINTS

Throughout this book you will find tips nestled within recipes. Those tips will apply to each specific dish, but before you get started, I want to give you some general cooking tips to help you feel empowered in your kitchen and ready to tackle any new recipe.

1. **Always read the recipe before starting:** And when you are done, reread the entire recipe. Knowing and understanding the directions and being familiar with a recipe will make the entire process run smoothly.

2. **Practice mise en place:** This French term means "everything in its place"—in other words, it means preparing and measuring all the ingredients for a recipe before you start cooking and organizing them neatly in your work space. When you have everything ready to go, you can focus on the recipe directions, leaving less room for error and omission.

3. **Invest in a good chef's knife:** A chef's knife is the one tool that you will use over and over. Making sure your knife is sharp is the key to fast, safe, and efficient prepping. Always be careful when using a knife.

4. **Use an instant-read meat thermometer:** Cooking meats to the proper temperature is incredibly important. To avoid bacteria and other microorganisms, ground beef and pork should be cooked to at least 160°F, steaks and pork chops to 145°F, and chicken and turkey to 165°F.

5. **Make notes about your recipes:** These recipes can be played with and adjusted to your own taste. When you find a recipe you love, circle it in the book! If you discover you need to cook something longer in your oven, make a note of it right on the recipe page. Anything you want to remember can and should be penciled in.

6. **Use spice blends:** Pick up, or make your own, spice blends. Taco Seasoning, Italian Seasoning, and Salad Sprinkle are just a few staples I always have on hand. See pages 156 to 157 for all my Quick and Easy Spice Seasonings.

7. **Do not crowd your pan:** Adding too many ingredients to a heated pan causes the temperature to drop drastically, which hinders the entire cooking process. Foods can steam instead of fry, or undercook because of the lower temperature, resulting in a dramatically different texture than expected. Work in batches, as needed, for best results.

8. **Invest in an enamel-coated Dutch oven or skillet:** This is not a requirement, but if you invest in only one kitchen tool, let it be an enamel-coated pan. Another great option is cast iron, which is optimal for even heat distribution and cooking and can be used on the stovetop or in the oven. It will be your most-used tool and will pay for itself in no time.

9. **Remember that recipes are only guidelines:** Feel free to adjust or to substitute items based on your tastes and what you have on hand. I include some suggestions in easily adaptable recipes throughout this book, but don't be afraid to test other ingredients and swap flavors to fit what you like.

LIGHTNING-QUICK CLEANUP

Cleaning up is a daunting task no one loves, but it comes with the joys of cooking. After years of practically living in my kitchen, I have developed a few tricks that make the cleaning process much easier. Here are a few of my favorite ways to keep things tidy and make cleanup a breeze.

1. **Clean as you go:** This tip is the easiest to incorporate into your routine. When you finish using a tool, set it in your sink and give it a quick rinse so it will be less of a mess to wash later. You can even start the cleanup process while your food cooks. This works best when you are comfortable with a recipe—don't feel any pressure to multitask cleaning and cooking when just starting out.

2. **Cook in one pan:** Cooking one pot/pan recipes, like my Garlic Parmesan Pasta (page 55), means less mess because everything is done in a single pot! You might need one or two utensils and a cutting board, but the wash load will still be much smaller than after using multiple cooking vessels.

3. **Use parchment paper:** Lining pans that go into the oven with parchment paper makes cleanup simple. When you are done cooking, remove the parchment paper and toss it into the trash. Washing your pan will be a breeze.

4. **Soak pans while you eat:** Toss your dirty pans into the sink to soak while you eat and enjoy your meal. Everything stuck to the pans will start to loosen and be ready for a simple final wash when you're done eating. For tougher messes, I spritz the slightly cooled pots and pans with a mixture of water and dish soap, then let them sit in the sink. When I'm ready to clean up, the tough mess practically wipes right out.

5. **Enlist help:** Ask someone to help you. Whether it is one of your children, your partner, spouse, or a friend, having that extra set of hands is always a bonus!

STOCKING THE KITCHEN

Keeping a well-stocked pantry and kitchen is a huge benefit when you cook. There are a few essentials you should always have on hand to help you whip up amazingly simple meals in no time. Having the proper food-storage containers and the best tools for cooking are the easiest ways to set yourself up for success.

Tools and Equipment

You do not need to have every crazy kitchen gadget available to be successful in the kitchen—though I do admit to owning more tortilla warmers than any one person needs. Many of my must-have kitchen favorites are basic and easy to use. They are items you use day in and day out, and you most likely already own at least some of them.

Must Have

Cutting board: I own a bamboo cutting board and find it is durable and easy to keep clean. However, there are many varieties of cutting boards to choose from, like plastic or silicone. Having a separate board to use just for meats is always a good idea.

Hand mixer: A hand mixer is an excellent addition to your kitchen appliances. Beaters are attached to an electric handheld attachment, which makes mixing doughs and batters super quick and simple.

Measuring cups and spoons: You should have a glass or high-quality plastic measuring cup to measure liquids. For dry ingredients, I recommend stainless steel cups and spoons that usually come in sets. These will last longer, and the measurements tend to be etched in the steel, which means they will not wear away with time.

Mixing bowls: For a long-lasting option, consider stainless steel mixing bowls. They are incredibly durable, and you will avoid chipping or shattering a glass bowl in the event of an accident. A three-bowl set with 1½-quart, 3-quart, and 5-quart bowls is perfect.

Oven-safe pot/pan: I will say it again, if you only can afford one oven-safe pot, make it an enamel-coated Dutch oven. It is versatile and easy to use, it is oven- and stovetop-safe, and it cooks food evenly. Stainless steel or cast-iron skillets work well, too.

Sharp knife set: You do not need to invest in a large knife set but consider purchasing a set that includes a chef's knife and a paring knife because you will use them frequently.

Slow cooker: This tool will become one of your go-to appliances for busy weeknight dinners. Slow cookers come in various sizes ranging from 1½-quarts to 8 quarts. For the recipes in this book, unless specifically stated otherwise, use a 4-quart slow cooker. This size is ideal for families of 4 to 6 people. If you use a slow cooker that's larger than 4 quarts, you may need to shorten the cook time or stir occasionally while cooking.

> **Slow cooker tip:** For slow cooker recipes that need a smaller cooking crock, like my Queso con Carne (page 122), place a small **oven-safe bowl** inside the slow cooker. Add the ingredients directly to the bowl and cook as directed.

Spatulas and other utensils: Silicone spatulas are the kings of my kitchen. Silicone is heat resistant, which means you can use them while cooking stovetop dishes as well as for folding batter for desserts. Also be sure to have a whisk, tongs, wooden spoon, and a slotted spatula in your collection.

Nice to Have

Airtight food-storage containers: Storing leftovers properly helps minimize food waste. Invest in a quality—preferably glass—storage set with varying sizes and lids.

Food processor: This tool is great for chopping vegetables, kneading dough, and even blending juices or sauces.

Immersion blender: An immersion blender can quickly and conveniently puree soups and sauces, blend smoothies, and even make whipped cream.

Stand mixer: A stand mixer is not a necessity, especially if you already own a hand mixer, but it is incredibly helpful when baking. We even use ours to shred chicken.

Staple Ingredients

The ingredients you keep in your kitchen do not have to be complex or expensive. Here are a few items that I always keep stocked. Adjust this list according to your family's preferences.

In Your Refrigerator

Butter: In our home, we always have both salted and unsalted butter on hand. I use salted butter when cooking unless a recipe specifically states otherwise.

Cheese: If you must pick only one cheese, make it Cheddar, which is versatile and can be used in many dishes. Parmesan and mozzarella are great options, as well.

Eggs: Eggs are a great source of protein and can be incorporated into every week's meal plan! Large eggs are the standard for this book's recipes.

Fruit and vegetables: If you find yourself throwing out more vegetables than you eat, purchase just one or two types of vegetables each for the week and make those veggies part of your meals. You will see less waste and find yourself getting more creative with how you incorporate vegetables into your diet. Good examples include onions and bell peppers, which are used throughout my recipes, as in the Potato, Pepper, and Cheese Breakfast Casserole (page 19), Cheesy Bacon Breakfast Burritos (page 16), Tomato and Bell Pepper Pasta Salad (page 43), and Southwest Stuffed Sweet Potatoes (page 60).

Milk: Buttermilk and whole milk are used for recipes in this book . . . and whole milk is good to have on hand for those nights when cereal sounds good for dinner.

In Your Freezer

Poultry, meat, and fish: These items could also go into the refrigerated section, but I prefer to freeze meats. They last longer and taste just as delicious as fresh. Remember to thaw what you need in the refrigerator for 24 hours before using.

Vegetables: If you are worried about using fresh vegetables before they expire, consider stocking up on frozen vegetables. They are just as tasty as fresh vegetables, they are easy to roast, they can be added to a recipe to boost the nutrition, and they can be served as a delicious side dish.

In Your Pantry

All-purpose flour and sugar: If you have a little of each of these items on hand, you can whip up a sweet treat in no time.

Bread: Any bread you prefer will work well for the recipes in this book. Within minutes, you can have a Garlic Butter Grilled Cheese (page 49) or a simple Bacon and Egg Breakfast Sandwich (page 20) on the table.

Broth, or broth base: I happen to be a big fan of Better Than Bouillon beef, chicken, and vegetable broth bases. They have a long shelf life and deliver the same great flavor as canned broth.

Dried herbs and spices: Salt, pepper, and other spices, like garlic powder and onion powder, are the keys to adding bold flavor to simple ingredients. Adding spice blends (see pages 156 to 157) can also be a huge flavor booster!

Jarred tomato sauce: The shelf life of tomato sauce is unbeatable. The recipes in this book go a long way toward making jarred sauce taste homemade.

Oils: Vegetable and canola oil are the most common cooking oils and they are interchangeable throughout this book. When purchasing olive oil, always go for the extra-virgin olive oil.
I also like avocado oil and avocado oil spray, which are flavorless, so they work well for both sweet and savory dishes.

Onions and garlic: These can always be found in my kitchen because they add such great flavor to so many dishes. Onions will last up to six weeks and garlic will last three to four months. Store both onions and garlic in a cool, dry, dark place for optimal longevity.

Pasta: You can find inexpensive dried pasta at most grocers. Stock your favorite varieties for a quick meal in a pinch. Easy Fettuccine Alfredo (page 58), anyone?

Rice: Adding rice to a recipe is one of the easiest ways to make it a full meal. Basmati rice is my pick. It has a mild nutty and floral flavor that pairs nicely with most dishes. You'll love it with my Orange Cauliflower Bowls (page 62).

HOW TO USE THIS BOOK

These recipes are for beginners and seasoned cooks alike. If you're new to the cooking game, you can always come back to this chapter for answers to any questions. Whether you are trying to improve your grocery shopping experience or master my top cooking tips, this book has you covered.

Cooking at home is a healthier alternative to eating out. Whatever type of meal you crave, this book is all you'll need to satisfy that craving. The 125 recipes in the following chapters are simple and delicious—and happen to be my family's favorites.

As you read the book, you will find recipe labels, dietary labels, and tips nestled into each recipe. Let me break those down so you can quickly find what you are looking for.

Recipe Labels

Every recipe is categorized according to the following:

- **5-Ingredient:** Sometimes less is more. These fuss-free recipes use only five ingredients (not counting salt, pepper, oil, and water), which means they're perfect for busy weeknights. By using fewer ingredients, you save prep time yet still have a flavorful meal the entire family will enjoy.

- **30-Minute:** Short on time? These meals can be made in 30 minutes or less from start to finish. That means you can have a tasty meal on the table in a flash. These recipes are some of my most frequently requested!

- **Make Ahead:** These recipes take the stress out of cooking. Prep beforehand and make a few of these recipes to keep in the refrigerator or freezer. Some, like soups, taste even better after sitting for a while as the flavors blend. When you find yourself short on time or inspiration, a satisfying meal can be as easy as heat and eat.

- **One Pot/Pan:** Hate doing dishes? I'm with you. Recipes in this category use one main pot or pan as a cooking vessel. A Dutch oven, skillet, or sheet pan is all that's necessary for recipes with this label.

You will need a few other cookware items (think spatula or measuring cups), but you'll avoid extensive cleanup and still get a flavor-packed meal.

- **Slow Cooker:** These recipes are for anyone looking for a dump-and-go-style recipe. They are ideal for anyone who wants a home-cooked meal with minimal effort. All the ingredients are combined in the main pot and cooked at a low temperature for a long time. If you have a busy day ahead or you are simply looking for a set-it-and-forget-it dish, this category is for you.

These labels will help you find what you need at a glance. Turn to pages 162 to 166 for a complete list of the recipes nestled under their respective labels.

Dietary Labels

- **Dairy-Free:** Contains no dairy
- **Gluten-Free:** Contains no gluten
- **Nut-Free:** Contains no nuts

Tips

- **Addition tip:** These tips include items you can add to the recipe to adjust the flavor or boost the nutrition of the dish.
- **Cooking tip:** These valuable tips will help ease and improve your cooking experience.
- **Ingredient tip:** These tips give you more information about how to use a specific ingredient in the recipe.
- **Make ahead tip:** These tips include instructions on how a recipe can be made in advance and served later.
- **Storage tip:** These tips are shared to ensure items are stored safely, which helps extend the life of your leftovers.
- **Variation tip:** These tips give you ways to customize the recipe according to your personal tastes.

I hope to spread my passion for simple recipes and good food to you and your family. Happy cooking!

BREAKFAST

< Bacon and Egg Breakfast Sandwiches, p. 20

BUTTERMILK PANCAKES

MAKES 12 SMALL OR 8 LARGE PANCAKES | PREP TIME: 10 MINUTES | COOK TIME: 20 MINUTES

30-MINUTE | MAKE AHEAD | NUT-FREE

There is nothing quite like homemade pancakes. The buttermilk adds a delightful tangy flavor, activates the baking soda, and breaks down the gluten to give you an incredibly light pancake. For the fluffiest pancakes, use room-temperature ingredients. I take my eggs and milk out of the refrigerator 20 minutes before starting.

1½ cups all-purpose flour

2 tablespoons sugar

1½ teaspoons baking powder

¾ teaspoon baking soda

¼ teaspoon kosher salt

1½ cups buttermilk

¼ cup whole milk

2 large eggs

3 tablespoons unsalted butter, melted, plus 1 teaspoon

½ teaspoon pure vanilla extract

Warm syrup and fresh fruit (optional), for serving

1. In a large bowl, whisk the flour, sugar, baking powder, baking soda, and salt to combine and set aside.

2. In a large measuring cup, stir together the buttermilk, whole milk, eggs, 3 tablespoons of melted butter, and vanilla. Pour the wet ingredients into the dry ingredients, folding just until incorporated. Do not overmix the batter.

3. Preheat a skillet over medium-low heat. Melt the remaining 1 teaspoon of butter in the skillet.

4. Scoop ½-cup portions of batter into the preheated pan. Cook for 2 to 3 minutes, or until bubbles begin to form on the top of each pancake. Carefully flip the pancakes and cook for 2 to 3 minutes more, or until golden brown. Repeat for another batch, or until the batter is gone. Serve with warm syrup or fresh fruit, if desired.

Ingredient tip: No buttermilk? In a pinch, combine 1 tablespoon vinegar and 1 cup milk. Let sit for 5 to 10 minutes before using instead of the buttermilk.

Make ahead tip: If you are making these ahead for meal prep, let the pancakes cool completely. Transfer the cooled pancakes to a freezer-safe container or zip-top bag and freeze for up to 1 to 2 months. To reheat, place 3 pancakes in a stack on a microwave-safe plate. Heat on high power for 30 seconds, flip the stack over, and heat for 30 seconds more.

CRISP AND FLUFFY WAFFLES

MAKES 8 WAFFLES | PREP TIME: 20 MINUTES | COOK TIME: 30 MINUTES

MAKE AHEAD | NUT-FREE

The perfect waffle should have a crispy exterior and a fluffy center. It can be a tricky combo to pull off. The key is achieving the right amount of air in the batter by separating the eggs and whipping just the whites into a stiff meringue. Gently folding the meringue into the batter just before cooking gives you a wonderfully light waffle that is also insanely delicious!

2 cups all-purpose flour

¼ cup sugar

3½ teaspoons baking powder

2 large eggs, separated

1½ cups whole milk

8 tablespoons (1 stick) unsalted butter, melted

1 teaspoon pure vanilla extract

Nonstick cooking spray

1. In a large bowl, stir together the flour, sugar, and baking powder to combine. Set aside.

2. In a large measuring cup, whisk the egg yolks, milk, melted butter, and vanilla to blend. Mix the wet ingredients into the dry ingredients just until combined. Do not overmix the batter.

3. In a small bowl, using a hand mixer, whip the egg whites until stiff peaks form. Gently fold the beaten whites into the batter just until incorporated.

4. Preheat a waffle iron according to the manufacturer's instructions and lightly mist it with cooking spray. Spoon ¾ cup of batter onto the heated surface. Cook according to the manufacturer's instructions, or until crispy and slightly browned. Repeat with the remaining batter.

Cooking tip: I make these waffles with a Belgian waffle iron, but I've used several different irons and they all work. Your yield may differ if you use a different size waffle iron.

Make ahead tip: Waffles can be made in advance and frozen for up to 4 months, stored in an airtight container or freezer-safe bag. Reheat in a 350°F oven for 10 minutes. When ready to eat, top with butter and syrup and enjoy.

BUTTERY HOMEMADE BISCUITS

MAKES 8 TO 12 BISCUITS | PREP TIME: 20 MINUTES | COOK TIME: 10 MINUTES

5-INGREDIENT | 30-MINUTE | NUT-FREE

These flaky biscuits taste sinfully delicious on their own or slathered with butter and jam. I often serve them with my Country Sausage Gravy (opposite page). The pair is a match made in heaven and one of the most requested breakfasts in our home.

2 cups all-purpose flour, plus more for dusting

1 tablespoon baking powder

½ teaspoon kosher salt

8 tablespoons (1 stick) cold salted butter, cut into pieces

1 cup buttermilk

1. Preheat the oven to 450°F. Line a baking sheet with parchment paper. Set aside.

2. In a large bowl, stir together the flour, baking powder, and salt.

3. Add the butter to the dry ingredients. Using 2 knives, cut the butter into the flour mixture until it resembles coarse crumbs. Fold in the buttermilk until combined.

4. Generously dust a clean work surface with flour and turn the dough out onto the flour. Using your hands, pat the dough into a 1-inch-thick round. Do not use a rolling pin. Fold the dough in half, on top of itself, and press it down to a ½-inch thickness.

5. Using a round cookie cutter, or a drinking glass (I use a 3-inch cutter), cut out rounds of dough and place them on the prepared baking sheet.

6. Bake for 10 minutes, or until golden brown, watching closely so the biscuits do not overbake.

Cooking tip: Biscuit dough needs to stay chilled before it bakes in order to develop its flaky layers. Handle the dough as little as possible. If your dough gets tacky or warm, chill it for 1 hour and resume making your biscuits.

COUNTRY SAUSAGE GRAVY

SERVES 4 | PREP TIME: 5 MINUTES | COOK TIME: 15 MINUTES

5-INGREDIENT | 30-MINUTE | NUT-FREE | ONE POT/PAN

Biscuits and gravy are Southern staples. Spoon this gravy over my Buttery Homemade Biscuits (opposite page) and serve them with a fried egg for a hearty and filling meal. We enjoy spicy breakfast sausage with this recipe, but any variety will work.

8 ounces breakfast sausage

1 to 2 tablespoons salted butter (optional)

¼ cup all-purpose flour

2 cups whole milk

Freshly ground black pepper (optional)

1. Heat a medium skillet over medium heat. Add the sausage and cook for about 5 minutes, or until crumbled and browned. The sausage should produce some fat; if it does not, add 1 to 2 tablespoons of butter to the skillet.

2. Stir the flour directly into the sausage until you no longer see any white streaks in the mixture.

3. Stir in the milk and cook the gravy for 2 to 3 minutes, or until the gravy has thickened slightly. Season with pepper (if using) before serving.

CHEESY BACON BREAKFAST BURRITOS

SERVES 4 | PREP TIME: 15 MINUTES | COOK TIME: 15 MINUTES

30-MINUTE | MAKE AHEAD | NUT-FREE

If you are looking for a breakfast that is filling and freezer-friendly, look no further. Add cooked sausage, ham, or sautéed vegetables as desired.

4 bacon slices

6 large eggs

2 tablespoons salsa

½ teaspoon kosher salt

¼ teaspoon freshly ground black pepper

2 tablespoons salted butter

4 large (10-inch) flour tortillas

½ cup shredded Cheddar cheese

1. In a large skillet over medium heat, cook the bacon for about 10 minutes, or until crisp, turning at least once. Remove the bacon from the skillet and chop into bite-size pieces. Set aside.

2. In a medium measuring cup, whisk the eggs and salsa until combined. Add the salt and pepper and whisk again.

3. Drain the bacon grease from the skillet by carefully pouring it into a heatproof container to be discarded once cooled. Return the skillet to medium heat and add the butter to melt. Pour the egg mixture into the heated pan and cook for 3 to 4 minutes. Remove from the heat.

4. Place the tortillas on a clean work surface and spoon an equal amount of the eggs into the middle of each tortilla. Sprinkle with cheese and bacon. Gently fold the tortillas into burritos.

Ingredient tip: Heat the tortillas in the microwave on high power for 10 to 15 seconds before filling to make folding easier.

Make ahead tip: To freeze your assembled burritos, wrap each one individually with plastic wrap and place in a freezer-safe zip-top bag. Freeze for up to 3 months. When ready to eat, remove the plastic and wrap your burrito in a damp paper towel. Microwave on high power for 2 minutes, or until heated through.

EASIEST OVERNIGHT OATS

SERVES 4 | PREP TIME: 15 MINUTES

5-INGREDIENT | MAKE AHEAD | NUT-FREE | ONE POT/PAN

Overnight oatmeal is ideal for busy weekdays when you need a grab-and-go breakfast or snack. This base recipe walks you through the process of making overnight oats with three simple ingredients. Consider adding 1 tablespoon honey or brown sugar for a touch of sweetness, 1 teaspoon chia seeds for crunch, or ⅓ cup yogurt for a more filling dish.

2 cups rolled oats

2 cups whole milk

2 teaspoons pure vanilla extract

Place 4 half-pint jars or containers on your counter. In each, combine ½ cup oats, ½ cup milk, and ½ teaspoon vanilla. Stir to combine. Secure the lids and refrigerate overnight, or for up to 4 days.

VARIATIONS

Banana–Chocolate Chip: Stir ½ ripe smashed banana and ¼ cup mini chocolate chips into each jar before refrigerating.

Blueberry-Coconut: Substitute coconut milk for the whole milk and add ¼ cup fresh blueberries to each container before refrigerating.

Strawberry Cheesecake: Stir ¼ cup chopped fresh strawberries, 2 tablespoons room-temperature cream cheese, and ¼ teaspoon freshly squeezed lemon juice into each jar before refrigerating.

Ingredient tip: If you make any of the suggested variations, use the freshest fruit possible.

SAUSAGE AND CHEESE BREAKFAST PIZZA

SERVES 4 | PREP TIME: 15 MINUTES | COOK TIME: 20 MINUTES

5-INGREDIENT | MAKE AHEAD | NUT-FREE

This recipe comes together quickly and is sure to be a hit with the entire family. I like to make it early in the week and keep leftovers stored in a zip-top bag. Leftover pizza lasts two to three days and can be warmed quickly in the microwave or oven.

1 pound store-bought refrigerated pizza dough

6 large eggs

¼ teaspoon kosher salt

⅛ teaspoon freshly ground black pepper

2 tablespoons salted butter

1 cup shredded Cheddar cheese

½ cup crumbled cooked breakfast sausage

1. Preheat the oven to 425°F.
2. Unroll the pizza dough onto a large baking sheet. Prebake according to the package directions, usually 6 to 8 minutes.
3. In a medium bowl, whisk the eggs, salt, and pepper to combine.
4. Heat a 10-inch skillet over medium heat. Add the butter to melt, swirling the skillet to coat the entire bottom. Pour the eggs into the prepared skillet. Cook for 3 to 4 minutes, or until the eggs are cooked and fluffy, stirring often to avoid burning. Spoon the eggs onto the prebaked pizza crust. Sprinkle with Cheddar cheese and sausage.
5. Bake for 8 to 10 minutes, or until the cheese is melted and the crust is golden.

Variation tip: This recipe also tastes delicious with bacon instead of the sausage and chopped scallion sprinkled on top.

POTATO, PEPPER, AND CHEESE BREAKFAST CASSEROLE

SERVES 6 | PREP TIME: 5 MINUTES | COOK TIME: 7 HOURS

GLUTEN-FREE | NUT-FREE | SLOW COOKER

This easy set-it-and-forget-it breakfast can be started right before you go to sleep and enjoyed when you wake up. I like to use diced ham, but this casserole is just as tasty with cooked bacon or breakfast sausage. Sprinkle it with scallions for a fancy finish, and serve it with a side of fresh fruit for a hearty meal.

Nonstick cooking spray

1 (28-ounce) bag frozen diced breakfast potatoes, thawed

1 pound cooked ham, diced

¼ cup sliced yellow onion

½ red bell pepper, seeded and chopped

½ green bell pepper, seeded and chopped

8 ounces sharp Cheddar cheese, shredded

12 large eggs

1 cup whole milk

Kosher salt

Freshly ground black pepper

1. Mist a 4- to 6-quart slow cooker with cooking spray. Arrange half the breakfast potatoes in a single layer in the prepared cooker. Top with half of the ham, onion, red bell pepper, green bell pepper, and Cheddar cheese. Repeat the layers.

2. In a large bowl, whisk the eggs and milk until combined. Season with salt and pepper. Pour the egg mixture over the layers.

3. Cover and cook on Low heat for 7 hours. Refrigerate leftovers in an airtight container for 2 to 3 days.

Cooking tip: Line the slow cooker with aluminum foil for easy cleanup.

BACON AND EGG BREAKFAST SANDWICHES

SERVES 4 | PREP TIME: 10 MINUTES | COOK TIME: 18 MINUTES

5-INGREDIENT | MAKE AHEAD | NUT-FREE

Make these sandwiches in advance and keep them stored in your freezer for busy mornings when you need a handheld breakfast-to-go.

Nonstick cooking spray

4 large eggs

Kosher salt

Freshly ground black pepper

4 English muffins

4 tablespoons (½ stick) salted butter

4 slices Cheddar cheese

4 thick-cut bacon slices, cooked

1. Preheat the oven to 350°F. Mist 4 cups of a nonstick muffin tin with cooking spray.

2. Crack 1 egg into each of the prepared cups taking care not to break the yolk. Season with salt and pepper.

3. Bake the eggs for 14 to 18 minutes, or until the whites are solid and the yolks are mostly set.

4. While the eggs bake, split and toast the English muffins. Spread each toasted half with 1 tablespoon butter.

5. Carefully remove the eggs from the muffin tin. Place 1 egg on the bottom half of each English muffin. Top each with 1 slice of cheese and 1 bacon slice. Place the other half of the English muffin on top of the sandwich.

Make ahead tip: Let the sandwiches cool. Wrap each sandwich in plastic wrap and place in an airtight container or freezer-safe zip-top bag. Refrigerate for up to 1 week or freeze for up to 2 months. When ready to eat, remove the plastic wrap. Wrap the sandwich in a damp paper towel and microwave on high power for 1 to 2 minutes, or until heated through.

Variation tip: Use your favorite bagel in place of the English muffins.

PEANUT BUTTER–BANANA BREAKFAST SMOOTHIE

SERVES 1 | PREP TIME: 10 MINUTES

5-INGREDIENT | 30-MINUTE | GLUTEN-FREE | NUT-FREE | ONE POT/PAN

Smoothies are a wonderful and healthy way to fill up. This recipe combines a powdered breakfast drink mix with the sweet flavor of banana and creamy protein of peanut butter. Filling, delicious, and quick. Did I mention it's also kid-approved?

½ cup ice

1 banana, frozen

¾ cup whole milk

2 tablespoons creamy peanut butter

1 (1.26-ounce) packet chocolate powdered breakfast nutrition mix (I like Carnation Breakfast Essentials)

In a high-powered blender, place the ice, banana, milk, peanut butter, and breakfast mix, in that order. Pulse 2 to 3 minutes, or until smooth. Pour into a glass and enjoy.

Ingredient tip: Use overripe bananas, if possible, for a bolder, sweeter flavor.

Variation tip: Substitute the same amount of chocolate protein powder for the breakfast mix.

ONE MUFFIN FOUR WAYS

MAKES 6 MUFFINS | PREP TIME: 10 MINUTES | COOK TIME: 18 MINUTES

MAKE AHEAD | NUT-FREE

This muffin base has endless possibilities: Stir in your favorite fruit, chocolates, or nuts. And sprinkling the muffins with coarse sugar before baking gives them an elegant bakery-style finish. The muffins can be frozen for up to three months.

Nonstick cooking spray (optional)

¾ cup plus 2 tablespoons all-purpose flour

½ teaspoon baking powder

½ teaspoon baking soda

¼ teaspoon kosher salt

4 tablespoons (½ stick) unsalted butter, at room temperature

¼ cup plus 2 tablespoons unsalted sugar

1 large egg

¼ cup sour cream

2 tablespoons whole milk

1 teaspoon pure vanilla extract

1. Preheat the oven to 375°F. Line a muffin tin with paper liners, or mist with cooking spray. Set aside.

2. In a medium bowl, whisk the flour, baking powder, baking soda, and salt to combine. Set aside.

3. In a large bowl, stir the butter and sugar by hand for 5 minutes or beat with a hand mixer for 2 minutes, until creamy and light. Beat in the egg until combined. Scrape the sides of the bowl and mix in the sour cream, milk, and vanilla.

4. Fold the dry ingredients into the wet ingredients just until incorporated. Spoon the batter into the prepared muffin cups, filling each cup three-fourths full.

5. Bake for 15 to 18 minutes, or until a toothpick inserted into the center of a muffin comes out clean.

VARIATIONS

Apple-Cinnamon Muffins: Whisk ½ teaspoon cinnamon and ⅛ teaspoon nutmeg into the dry ingredients. Fold ½ cup diced peeled apple into the batter before filling the muffin tin.

Lemon-Glazed Berry Muffins: Fold ½ cup berries into the batter before filling the muffin tin. Bake as directed. Top with a glaze made with ½ cup powdered sugar and 1½ teaspoons to 1 tablespoon fresh lemon juice.

Chocolate Chip Muffins: Add ¼ teaspoon cinnamon to the dry ingredients and fold in ½ cup chocolate chips before filling the muffin tin.

ORANGE FRENCH TOAST

SERVES 4 | PREP TIME: 15 MINUTES | COOK TIME: 25 MINUTES

5-INGREDIENT | NUT-FREE

Is there anything better than French toast for breakfast? Thickly sliced bread dipped in a custard base, fried to a beautiful golden color, and served with butter and warm maple syrup is the definition of indulgence. Orange zest sets this recipe apart from the rest and takes the flavors to the next level.

4 large eggs

¼ cup whole milk, heavy (whipping) cream, or half-and-half

1 tablespoon honey

2 teaspoons grated orange zest

Nonstick cooking spray

8 thick-cut bread slices

1. In a shallow dish, whisk the eggs, milk, honey, and orange zest until the eggs have completely combined with the milk.
2. Heat a 10-inch skillet over medium heat. Mist with cooking spray.
3. Dip 1 slice of bread into the egg mixture, covering both sides. Let the excess custard drip back into the dish, then place the bread in the heated skillet. Cook for 1 to 2 minutes, or until golden. Flip and cook for 1 to 2 minutes more. Repeat with the remaining bread slices. Serve with butter and syrup, or as desired.

Addition tip: Add 1 teaspoon ground cinnamon and ¼ teaspoon pure vanilla extract to the batter for a cinnamon-spiced version.

Ingredient tip: Day-old bread soaks up the custard better and gives you soft, chewy French toast. I like to use thick-sliced French or challah bread.

QUICK AND EASY CHEESY OMELET

SERVES 1 | PREP TIME: 5 MINUTES | COOK TIME: 1 TO 2 MINUTES

5-INGREDIENT | 30-MINUTE | GLUTEN-FREE | MAKE AHEAD | NUT-FREE | ONE POT/PAN

This easy microwave omelet takes less than five minutes and tastes incredible! All you need are a few basic ingredients. Remember, every microwave will cook at a different rate, so I recommend checking the eggs every 30 seconds to ensure they do not burn.

Nonstick cooking spray

2 large eggs

Kosher salt

Freshly ground black pepper

1 tablespoon whole milk

2 tablespoons shredded cheese of choice

1 to 2 teaspoons each of a desired topping (such as diced ham, diced bell pepper, diced onion, or cooked bacon)

1. Lightly mist a small microwave-safe bowl with cooking spray. Crack both eggs into the prepared bowl. Season with salt and pepper. Whisk in the milk until the eggs are completely blended. Sprinkle with cheese and toppings as desired.

2. Microwave on high power for 30 seconds. Remove from the microwave and stir. Microwave for 30 seconds more. Stir the egg mixture and repeat until the eggs are fully cooked, roughly another 30 seconds to 1 minute. The eggs should be light and fluffy with no liquid remaining.

Make ahead tip: For an even faster breakfast, make omelet freezer packs in advance. Chop toppings and store them in freezer-safe zip-top bags. Pull a pack out of the freezer when you are ready to make your omelet and sprinkle shredded cheese and the toppings on the eggs before microwaving.

CRUNCHY VANILLA GRANOLA

SERVES 4 | PREP TIME: 15 MINUTES | COOK TIME: 40 MINUTES

DAIRY-FREE | MAKE AHEAD

This delicious vanilla granola makes your home smell scrumptious while it bakes! Eat it as snack or as breakfast, either by the handful or over yogurt with fresh fruit. Consider mixing in toasted nuts, dried fruit, or seeds for added flavor and texture.

3 cups rolled oats

¼ cup packed light brown sugar

½ teaspoon kosher salt

¼ teaspoon ground cinnamon

⅓ cup coconut oil

⅓ cup honey

4 teaspoons pure vanilla extract

1. Preheat the oven to 300°F. Line a baking sheet with a silicone baking mat or parchment paper. Set aside.

2. In a medium bowl, stir together the oats, brown sugar, salt, and cinnamon and set aside.

3. In a medium saucepan, whisk together the coconut oil and honey over medium heat just until warmed and the oil is completely melted. Remove from the heat and stir in the vanilla.

4. Add the oat mixture to the vanilla-honey coconut oil and stir until coated. Spread the granola on the prepared baking sheet.

5. Bake for 15 minutes, stir, and bake for 15 minutes more, or until the granola is golden brown and fragrant.

6. Cool completely, then store in an airtight container or jar at room temperature for up to 1 month.

Variation tip: Substitute an equal amount of vegetable oil or canola oil for the coconut oil.

PERFECTLY FLUFFY SCRAMBLED EGGS

SERVES 2 | PREP TIME: 5 MINUTES | COOK TIME: 8 MINUTES

5-INGREDIENT | 30-MINUTE | GLUTEN-FREE | NUT-FREE | ONE POT/PAN

My method for making fluffy, flavorful scrambled eggs is simple, but it produces incredibly delicious results. The secret is to constantly move the eggs in the pan. Eggs cook extremely quickly, so removing them from the heat at the right time produces the best scrambled eggs. Though simple, the technique takes a bit of practice. Once you master it, there is no going back.

4 large eggs

1 tablespoon water

Kosher salt

Freshly ground black pepper

1 tablespoon unsalted butter

1. Crack the eggs into a medium bowl. Add the water and season with salt and pepper. Whisk the eggs for about 1 minute, making sure the egg yolks and whites are mixed well and the seasonings are evenly distributed.

2. Heat an 8- to 10-inch skillet over medium-low heat. Add the butter to melt, tilting the skillet so it fully coats the bottom.

3. Pour the whisked eggs into the skillet. Using a silicone spatula, gently pull the outside of the eggs toward the center. Gently mix the eggs, constantly moving your spatula back and forth until the uncooked eggs no longer flood the empty areas of the skillet. Continue folding the scrambled eggs just until finished cooking and no liquid is apparent. Remove from the heat and serve immediately.

VARIATIONS

Cheesy Bacon Eggs: Add 3 slices cooked, crumbled bacon immediately after pouring the eggs into the skillet. Cook as directed. Sprinkle with shredded cheese before serving.

Southwest Scramble: Substitute 1 tablespoon sour cream for the water. In the heated skillet, combine ¼ cup diced onion and ¼ cup diced bell pepper. Cook for 3 to 5 minutes. Pour the beaten eggs over the vegetables and cook as directed. Sprinkle with shredded cheese before serving.

Spinach and Mushroom: Put ¼ cup fresh spinach and 2 tablespoons diced mushroom in the heated skillet. Cook for 1 to 2 minutes, or until the vegetables are soft. Add the eggs and cook as directed.

SOUPS AND SALADS

< Italian Sausage Lasagna Soup, p. 31

BROCCOLI CHEESE SOUP

SERVES 4 | PREP TIME: 10 MINUTES | COOK TIME: 20 MINUTES

5-INGREDIENT | 30-MINUTE | GLUTEN-FREE | MAKE AHEAD | NUT-FREE | ONE POT/PAN

This broccoli cheese soup is comfort food at its finest—and if you ask my sister, it is the best soup ever. Light, delicious, creamy cheese is melted into a tasty broccoli soup. Feel free to add 1 cup diced cooked ham for a flavor twist, or garnish it with crumbled bacon and freshly shredded cheese.

3½ cups water

2 (10.5-ounce) cans cream of chicken soup

½ cup diced onion

2 large russet potatoes, peeled and chopped into 1-inch pieces

2 (12-ounce) bags frozen broccoli florets

1 (16-ounce) package Velveeta cheese, diced

1. In a large saucepan, whisk the water and soup to combine. Stir in the onion and potatoes and bring to a boil over medium heat. Reduce the heat to low and simmer for 10 minutes.

2. Stir in the frozen broccoli and cook for 10 minutes more, or until the potatoes are fork-tender. Remove from the heat and stir in the cheese. Serve hot.

3. Cool any leftovers, then refrigerate in an airtight container for 2 to 3 days.

Ingredient tip: If using fresh broccoli, you will need 3 to 4 cups chopped broccoli florets.

ITALIAN SAUSAGE LASAGNA SOUP

SERVES 4 | PREP TIME: 15 MINUTES | COOK TIME: 35 MINUTES

MAKE AHEAD | NUT-FREE | ONE POT/PAN

Lasagna can be a labor of love, but the work is worth it for a beautiful layered pasta dish packed with flavor. This soup has lasagna's hearty components, but it can be made quickly in only one pot. Serve it with a sprinkle of fresh basil, a dollop of ricotta, and my Easy Baked Garlic Bread (page 118) on the side.

10 lasagna noodles, each noodle broken into 2 or 3 pieces

1 pound Italian sausage

1 cup diced onion

3 garlic cloves, minced

1 tablespoon Italian Seasoning (page 156) or store-bought seasoning

2 tablespoons tomato paste

3 cups chicken broth

1 (28-ounce) can diced tomatoes, undrained

⅓ cup grated Parmesan cheese

¼ cup half-and-half

Ricotta cheese, for serving

Fresh basil, for serving

1. Cook the lasagna noodles according to the package directions until al dente. Drain and set aside while preparing the rest of the soup.

2. In a large pot, combine the sausage and onion. Cook over medium heat for 8 to 10 minutes, stirring, until the onion is translucent and the sausage is crumbled and browned. Add the garlic and cook for 1 minute more, until fragrant.

3. Stir in the Italian seasoning, tomato paste, chicken broth, and tomatoes and their juices. Bring to a boil. Reduce the heat to low and simmer the soup for 10 minutes.

4. Stir in the Parmesan cheese and half-and-half. Simmer for 10 minutes more.

5. Add the cooked noodles. Divide the soup among 4 individual bowls and top with a dollop of ricotta and a sprinkling of fresh basil.

6. This soup will keep, refrigerated in an airtight container, for 2 to 3 days.

Variation tip: This recipe is also delicious with ground beef instead of sausage.

CLASSIC CHICKEN NOODLE SOUP

SERVES 4 | PREP TIME: 15 MINUTES | COOK TIME: 6 TO 8 HOURS

DAIRY-FREE | MAKE AHEAD | NUT-FREE | SLOW COOKER

Is there anything more comforting than chicken noodle soup? I remember my grandma serving this recipe on chilly winter days or when we were feeling under the weather, and it always brightened my day. This version calls for rotisserie chicken, but you could also use 1 pound of cooked chicken breasts.

1 cup chopped onion

1 cup sliced carrot

1 cup sliced celery

2 garlic cloves, minced

1 bay leaf

2 teaspoons kosher salt

½ teaspoon freshly ground black pepper

½ teaspoon dried thyme

5¾ cups chicken broth

1 rotisserie chicken, meat removed from the bones and diced

2 cups egg noodles

1 to 2 tablespoons chopped fresh parsley (optional)

1. In a 4- to 6-quart slow cooker, combine the onion, carrot, celery, garlic, bay leaf, salt, pepper, and thyme. Cover with the chicken broth. Top with the chicken.

2. Cover and cook on Low heat for 6 to 8 hours.

3. Just before serving, cook the noodles according to the package directions until al dente. Drain and stir the cooked noodles into the soup. Re-cover and cook for 5 minutes more, or until heated.

4. Remove the bay leaf before serving. Serve topped with fresh parsley (if using).

5. Cool leftovers, then refrigerate in an airtight container for 2 to 3 days.

Cooking tip: This recipe offers that classic flavor everyone loves. For a bolder chicken taste, add 2 teaspoons chicken bouillon base to the broth at the start of cooking.

UPGRADED GARLIC AND EGG INSTANT RAMEN

SERVES 2 | PREP TIME: 10 MINUTES | COOK TIME: 10 MINUTES

30-MINUTE | DAIRY-FREE | NUT-FREE | ONE POT/PAN

I would like to say we were thrifty when we were first married, but the reality was we were poor. We were young, in love, just starting out in the world, and always looking for ways to pinch pennies. This upgraded ramen recipe was created more than 12 years ago and has been a staple in our family ever since because it's inexpensive, quick, easy, and tasty!

4 cups chicken broth, unsalted or low-sodium

1 (3-ounce) package chicken-flavored instant ramen

½ cup chopped scallions, greens and whites separated

1 garlic clove, minced

1 teaspoon soy sauce

⅛ to ¼ teaspoon red pepper flakes

2 large eggs, whisked

Chili sauce, such as sriracha, for garnish

1. In a 4-quart saucepan, combine the chicken broth, ramen noodles, ramen seasoning packet, scallion whites, garlic, soy sauce, and red pepper flakes. Bring to a boil and cook for 2 minutes.

2. Stir in the eggs and cook for 1 minute, or until the eggs have cooked through.

3. Divide the soup between 2 bowls and sprinkle with the scallion greens. Season with chili sauce. Serve immediately.

Addition tip: Add 1 cup cooked diced chicken with the eggs for a little extra protein.

CHICKEN AND MUSHROOM THAI-STYLE COCONUT SOUP

SERVES 4 | PREP TIME: 15 MINUTES | COOK TIME: 10 MINUTES

30-MINUTE | DAIRY-FREE | GLUTEN-FREE | MAKE AHEAD | ONE POT/PAN

This version of Thai-style coconut soup is incredibly simple to make. The jalapeño pepper adds a touch of heat and the coconut cream adds a slightly sweet finish. I prefer to make this with chicken, but my mom frequently substitutes cooked shrimp.

1 teaspoon coconut oil

1 jalapeño pepper, seeded and diced

1½ tablespoons minced peeled fresh ginger

¾ cup sliced mushrooms

1 cup chopped cooked chicken

3½ cups chicken broth

1¾ cups coconut cream

½ teaspoon kosher salt

Juice of 1 lime

¼ cup sliced scallions

1. In a medium pot, heat the oil over medium heat. Add the jalapeño pepper, ginger, and mushrooms. Cook for 2 minutes, or until soft.

2. Stir in the chicken, chicken broth, coconut cream, and salt. Bring to a boil. Reduce the heat to low and simmer the soup for 3 minutes.

3. Stir in the lime juice. Serve topped with scallions.

4. Cool any leftovers, then refrigerate in an airtight container for 2 to 3 days.

EASY HOMEMADE TOMATO SOUP

SERVES 4 | PREP TIME: 10 MINUTES | COOK TIME: 1 HOUR 15 MINUTES

GLUTEN-FREE | MAKE AHEAD | NUT-FREE | ONE POT/PAN

Homemade tomato soup and Garlic Butter Grilled Cheese (page 49) has been a staple in my home for years. My husband calls this the perfect soup and always brings us a bowl when we need some comfort. For the tomatoes, I recommend using San Marzano, but any canned variety will work.

2 tablespoons extra-virgin olive oil

1 onion, thinly sliced

¾ cup shredded carrot

2 garlic cloves, minced

2 (28-ounce) cans whole tomatoes, undrained

3 cups vegetable broth or chicken broth

1 teaspoon kosher salt

¼ teaspoon red pepper flakes

¼ cup grated Parmesan cheese (optional)

1. In a medium pot, heat the oil over medium heat. Add the onion and carrot. Cook, stirring frequently to prevent browning, for 3 to 5 minutes, or until soft. Stir in the garlic and cook for 1 minute more, until fragrant.

2. Stir in the tomatoes and their juices, the broth, salt, and red pepper flakes. Increase the heat to medium-high and bring the soup to a boil. Reduce the heat to low and simmer the soup for 1 hour, uncovered.

3. Let the soup cool slightly, then carefully pour the soup into a blender and pulse until the vegetables are smooth. Vent the lid while pulsing to avoid pressure buildup. Transfer the soup back to the pot and stir in the Parmesan cheese (if using).

4. Cool leftovers, then refrigerate in an airtight container for 3 to 4 days.

Cooking tip: If you have an immersion blender use it to blend the soup directly in the pot.

TUSCAN-STYLE SAUSAGE AND KALE SOUP

SERVES 6 | PREP TIME: 10 MINUTES | COOK TIME: 3 TO 6 HOURS

GLUTEN-FREE | MAKE AHEAD | NUT-FREE | SLOW COOKER

This soup is light, filling, and packed with flavor. Sausage is cooked and combined with potato and kale and finished with crumbled bacon. This soup pairs wonderfully with a simple side salad with Italian Salad Dressing (page 148) or my Easy Baked Garlic Bread (page 118).

1 pound bulk Italian sausage

1 to 2 teaspoons red pepper flakes (optional)

3 garlic cloves, minced

½ large onion, chopped

3 large russet potatoes, washed but not peeled, cut into large pieces

5½ cups chicken broth

1¾ cups water

4 cups thinly sliced kale

1 cup half-and-half

4 bacon slices, cooked and crumbled

1. Heat a 10-inch skillet over medium heat. Cook the sausage and red pepper flakes (if using) for 8 to 10 minutes, stirring frequently, or until the sausage is crumbled and browned. Transfer the sausage to a 4- to 6-quart slow cooker. Add the garlic, onion, potatoes, chicken broth, and water in that order.

2. Cover and cook on High heat for 3 to 4 hours, or on Low heat for 5 to 6 hours.

3. About 30 minutes before serving, stir in the kale and half-and-half. Cover and cook for the remaining 30 minutes, or until heated through. Stir in the bacon just before serving and enjoy.

4. Cool leftovers, then refrigerate in an airtight container for 2 to 3 days.

Cooking tip: To cook this on the stovetop, brown the sausage in a Dutch oven or large pot as directed. Add the garlic, onion, potatoes, and chicken broth. Simmer for 30 minutes, or until the potatoes are soft. Stir in the kale and half-and-half and cook for 5 minutes more, or until the kale is soft. Serve topped with bacon.

BEEF VEGETABLE SOUP

SERVES 4 TO 6 | PREP TIME: 10 MINUTES | COOK TIME: 8 HOURS

DAIRY-FREE | NUT-FREE | SLOW COOKER

My beef vegetable soup is hearty, filling, and easy to make. All the ingredients are combined in a slow cooker and simmered for 8 hours, blending the flavors into the most incredibly delicious soup. Serve on its own or over mashed potatoes.

1 pound beef stew meat

1 (14.5-ounce) can green beans, undrained

1 (14.5-ounce) can carrots, undrained

1 (14.5-ounce) can crushed tomatoes

2 large russet potatoes, peeled and cubed

1 cup frozen corn kernels

3 tablespoons Onion Soup Mix (page 157), or 1 (1.25-ounce) packet onion soup mix

3 garlic cloves, minced

1. In a 4- to 6-quart slow cooker, combine all the ingredients.
2. Cover and cook on Low heat for 8 hours.
3. Cool leftovers, then refrigerate in an airtight container for 3 to 4 days.

Cooking tip: This recipe does best when cooked for the full 8 hours. Stew meat needs that entire time to reach the soft, fall-apart texture you want.

GREEK SALAD WITH LEMON-GARLIC DRESSING

SERVES 4 | PREP TIME: 20 MINUTES

30-MINUTE | GLUTEN-FREE | NUT-FREE

A Greek salad is a wonderful dish to serve in summer or early fall, since fresh tomatoes and cucumbers are at their peak from May to October. In a twist on the traditional salad, this version relies only on vegetables and contains no lettuce.

½ cup extra-virgin olive oil

¼ cup red wine vinegar

2 tablespoons freshly squeezed lemon juice (from about 1 lemon)

2 garlic cloves, minced

1½ teaspoons Dijon mustard

½ teaspoon dried basil

¼ teaspoon dried oregano

¼ teaspoon salt

1 cucumber, seeded and sliced

1 red bell pepper or green bell pepper, seeded and diced

1¼ cups cherry tomatoes, halved

½ red onion, sliced

½ cup pitted olives

1 cup crumbled feta cheese

1. In a medium screw-top jar, combine the olive oil, vinegar, lemon juice, garlic, mustard, basil, oregano, and salt. Seal the lid and shake well to combine. Set aside.

2. In a medium bowl, combine the cucumber, bell pepper, tomatoes, red onion, olives, and feta cheese. Drizzle with the dressing and gently toss to combine.

Cooking tip: The dressing can be made up to 5 days ahead and kept refrigerated until needed.

STRAWBERRY SPINACH SALAD

SERVES 4 | PREP TIME: 15 MINUTES

5-INGREDIENT | 30-MINUTE | GLUTEN-FREE | ONE POT/PAN

This salad is amazingly simple and so fresh. Spinach replaces lettuce and fresh berries add a sweetness that complements the vinaigrette. I use strawberries, but feel free to swap them for any in-season berry for equally delicious results. I often serve this as a side for Go-To Grilled Chicken (page 72) or Foil-Baked Salmon with Dill (page 81).

5 cups baby spinach, washed and dried

2 cups strawberries, hulled and sliced

½ cup roasted pecans

¼ cup crumbled feta cheese (optional)

½ cup Balsamic Vinaigrette (page 147) or store-bought raspberry vinaigrette

1. In a large bowl, place the spinach, strawberries, and pecans. Top with the feta (if using).
2. Drizzle with the vinaigrette and gently toss to combine. Serve immediately.

Cooking tip: Use an egg slicer to slice the strawberries quickly and evenly.

BROCCOLI PASTA SALAD

SERVES 4 | PREP TIME: 20 MINUTES, PLUS AT LEAST 1 HOUR TO CHILL | COOK TIME: 15 MINUTES

MAKE AHEAD

Broccoli is one vegetable that is never underutilized in my kitchen. It is easy to add to almost any dish and keeps for long periods in the refrigerator. This pasta salad takes full advantage of that quality and can be made up to four days in advance. The longer this salad sits, the better the flavors become. It's ideal for summer gatherings or potlucks.

1 (9-ounce) package cheese tortellini

3½ cups broccoli florets, cut into bite-size pieces

¼ red onion, diced

6 tablespoons dried cranberries or raisins

6 tablespoons sliced almonds, toasted

4 bacon slices, cooked and crumbled

½ cup mayonnaise

¼ cup sugar

1 tablespoon apple cider vinegar

1. Cook the tortellini according to the package directions until al dente. Drain and let cool while preparing the rest of the salad.

2. In a large bowl, stir together the broccoli, red onion, dried cranberries, almonds, and bacon.

3. Add the cooled pasta and gently mix it into the other ingredients.

4. In a small measuring cup, whisk the mayonnaise, sugar, and vinegar together. Pour the dressing over the salad and gently toss to combine. Refrigerate for 1 to 2 hours before serving.

ITALIAN CHOPPED SALAD

SERVES 4 | PREP TIME: 20 MINUTES
30-MINUTE | GLUTEN-FREE | NUT-FREE

This salad came about on a hot summer day when I could not bear the idea of turning on the oven. This chopped salad is quick to make, and when you add a hefty dose of protein and veggies, it can be incredibly filling! I often serve this with Italian Salad Dressing (page 148), but you can also try my Homemade Ranch Dressing (page 146) for a taste variation.

3 cups chopped romaine lettuce

2 tomatoes, chopped

¾ cup chopped pepperoni

½ cup chopped deli ham

½ cup peperoncini, diced

½ cup chopped cucumber

1 (3.8-ounce) can sliced olives, drained

¼ large red onion, sliced or chopped

¼ cup Italian Salad Dressing (page 148) or Homemade Ranch Dressing (page 146)

2 to 3 tablespoons grated Parmesan cheese

1. In a large bowl, combine the lettuce, tomatoes, pepperoni, ham, peperoncini, cucumber, olives, and red onion. Drizzle with the dressing and toss to combine.

2. Sprinkle with Parmesan before serving.

Cooking tip: This recipe is easy to customize. Add your favorite salad toppings or swap in your favorite dressing—don't be afraid to get creative!

BEEF TACO SALAD

SERVES 4 | PREP TIME: 15 MINUTES | COOK TIME: 15 MINUTES

30-MINUTE | NUT-FREE

This flavorful taco salad is made with seasoned ground beef, chopped lettuce, and all your favorite taco toppings. Ready in about 30 minutes, it's the perfect weeknight dinner. Although the traditional dressing for a taco salad is Catalina, my family prefers my Homemade Ranch Dressing (page 146).

1 pound ground beef

1 cup diced onion

2 tablespoons Taco Seasoning (page 156) or store-bought seasoning

¼ cup water

2 large heads romaine lettuce, chopped

2 tomatoes, diced

2 cups shredded Cheddar cheese or pepper Jack cheese

1 cup canned corn, drained and rinsed

½ cup sliced olives

2 to 4 tablespoons sliced scallion greens

1 (15-ounce) bag Cheddar cheese–flavored tortilla chips

½ cup Homemade Ranch Dressing (page 146)

1. Heat a large skillet over medium heat. Add the ground beef and onion and cook for 8 to 10 minutes, until the onion is translucent and the beef is crumbled and browned. Stir in the taco seasoning and water. Cook for 2 minutes, or until warmed through.

2. Build each salad by placing the lettuce in a large bowl and topping with the beef mixture, tomatoes, cheese, corn, olives, scallion greens, and a sprinkle of slightly crushed tortilla chips.

3. Drizzle with ranch dressing to serve.

Ingredient tip: You'll have leftover whole tortilla chips. Go ahead and serve them on the side!

TOMATO AND BELL PEPPER PASTA SALAD

SERVES 4 | PREP TIME: 20 MINUTES | COOK TIME: 10 MINUTES

30-MINUTE | DAIRY-FREE | MAKE AHEAD | NUT-FREE

My mom would make this recipe with spaghetti noodles for every summer potluck we attended. It was my absolute favorite side dish. I have slightly adapted the ingredients, but her method is the same.

3 tablespoons Salad Sprinkle (page 156), or store-bought salad seasoning mix

½ cup Italian Salad Dressing (page 148), or store-bought dressing, plus more as needed

8 ounces spiral pasta

1 cup cherry tomatoes, halved

1 cup chopped green bell pepper

½ cup chopped yellow bell pepper

½ cup shredded carrot

¼ cup diced celery

¼ cup diced red onion

¼ cup sliced pitted olives

1. In a medium bowl, whisk the salad seasoning and Italian dressing together.
2. Cook pasta until al dente, according to package directions. Drain.
3. Add the cooked pasta, tomatoes, green and yellow bell peppers, carrot, celery, red onion, and olives. Gently toss to combine. Refrigerate until ready to serve.
4. Serve cold. Add more Italian dressing, if needed.
5. Refrigerate leftovers in an airtight container for up to 4 days.

Cooking tip: Although this salad can be enjoyed immediately, make it ahead to let the flavors marinate in the fridge. I like to make it the night before serving.

CHEF'S SALAD WITH TURKEY, BACON, AND HAM

SERVES 4 | PREP TIME: 20 MINUTES
30-MINUTE | GLUTEN-FREE | NUT-FREE

This chef's salad is the ultimate 30-minute meal. Crisp romaine lettuce, delicious deli-sliced meat, and fresh vegetables combine to make this a super-simple, yet filling meal.

5 cups chopped romaine lettuce

½ cup chopped oven-roasted deli turkey

½ cup chopped deli ham

4 bacon slices, cooked and crumbled

½ cup chopped Swiss or Cheddar cheese

½ cup cherry tomatoes, halved

1 cucumber, peeled and sliced

4 hard-boiled eggs, peeled and quartered

¼ cup diced red onion

1 cup salad dressing of choice (see Ingredient tip)

1. Divide the lettuce equally into 4 large bowls or plates.
2. Top each salad with equal amounts of turkey, ham, bacon, cheese, tomatoes, cucumber, egg, and red onion.
3. Drizzle each salad with dressing and enjoy.

Ingredient tip: This salad is delicious topped with my Homemade Ranch Dressing (page 146), Thousand Island dressing, or even Balsamic Vinaigrette (page 147).

VEGETARIAN AND VEGAN MAINS

< Personal Margherita Pizzas, p. 56

GARLIC MUSHROOM FRIED RICE

SERVES 4 | PREP TIME: 15 MINUTES | COOK TIME: 35 MINUTES

DAIRY-FREE | MAKE AHEAD | NUT-FREE

This fried rice is packed full of my favorite vegetables and may be your new favorite meatless Monday meal. If you prepare the rice in advance, the dish can come together quickly and keeps for 5 to 7 days in the refrigerator. Feel free to add 1 pound chopped cooked chicken or ham for extra protein if you're not feeding vegetarians!

1½ cups basmati rice

2 teaspoons sesame oil

1 small yellow onion, diced

1 small green bell pepper, seeded and diced

½ cup matchstick carrots

½ cup diced mushrooms

1 teaspoon minced garlic

3 scallions, diced

1 cup frozen peas

3 tablespoons soy sauce

¼ teaspoon red pepper flakes

2 large eggs, whisked (optional)

1. Cook the rice according to the package directions.

2. In a large skillet or wok, heat the oil over medium heat. Add the onion, bell pepper, and carrots and cook for 3 minutes, stirring to avoid burning, until softened. Stir in the mushrooms and garlic and cook for 1 minute more.

3. Increase the heat to medium-high. Stir in the cooked rice, scallions, peas, soy sauce, and red pepper flakes. Cook for 1 minute, or until the peas are heated through.

4. If adding the eggs, push the rice mixture to the side of the skillet. Pour the eggs into the empty space and gently scramble for 2 minutes, or until cooked through. Mix the eggs into the rice and serve.

Ingredient tip: Vegetable oil can be used in place of the sesame oil, but you will lose a bit of flavor.

GARLIC BUTTER GRILLED CHEESE

SERVES 2 | PREP TIME: 5 MINUTES | COOK TIME: 10 MINUTES

5-INGREDIENT | 30-MINUTE | NUT-FREE

This recipe takes your everyday grilled cheese to a new level with delicious garlic butter, giving it a flavor-packed finish. An easy comfort meal ready in about 15 minutes, it pairs incredibly well with my Easy Homemade Tomato Soup (page 35). Add even more flavor to your sandwich by adding grilled vegetables—zucchini, red onion, and red bell pepper are some of my favorites.

2 tablespoons Garlic Butter
(page 150)

4 slices French bread

6 slices mild or medium
Cheddar cheese

1. Spread 1½ teaspoons of garlic butter onto one side of each bread slice.

2. Place 2 pieces of bread, buttered-side down, on a clean work surface. Layer each of 2 bread slices with 3 slices of cheese and top the sandwiches with the remaining bread slices, buttered-side up.

3. Heat a skillet over medium heat. Place one sandwich into the hot skillet and cook for 2 minutes per side, or until golden brown and the cheese is melted. Repeat with the second sandwich.

Addition tip: This is one of my favorite easy dinners. If we are eating meat, we often include two slices of ham or turkey on the sandwiches for added protein.

BLACK BEAN–CORN BURRITO BOWLS

SERVES 4 | PREP TIME: 15 MINUTES | COOK TIME: 15 MINUTES
30-MINUTE | DAIRY-FREE | GLUTEN-FREE | NUT-FREE

This simple burrito bowl is full of incredible flavor. Black beans are simmered and served over cooked quinoa and topped with pan-cooked vegetables. The result is a Mexican-inspired meal that is tailor-made for taco Tuesday.

½ cup quinoa, rinsed well

1 (15-ounce) can black beans, drained and rinsed

½ teaspoon garlic powder

¼ teaspoon chili powder

Pinch cayenne pepper

1 tablespoon vegetable oil

¼ cup diced yellow onion

1 red bell pepper, seeded and diced

1 cup frozen corn

1 avocado, sliced

Juice of 1 lime

Fresh cilantro, for garnish

Kosher salt

Freshly ground black pepper

1. Cook the quinoa according to the package directions. Set aside.
2. When the quinoa is almost done, in a small saucepan, combine the black beans, garlic powder, chili powder, and cayenne. Bring to a simmer over medium heat.
3. While the beans are heating, in an 8- to 10-inch skillet, heat the oil over medium heat. Add the onion and red bell pepper and cook for about 3 minutes, until softened. Add the frozen corn and cook for 1 to 2 minutes more, or until heated through.
4. Divide the cooked quinoa between 2 bowls. Top with the black beans and the vegetable mixture.
5. Garnish with avocado, lime juice, fresh cilantro, and salt and pepper.

Addition tip: For even more flavor, I sometimes serve this burrito bowl with Homemade Ranch Dressing (page 146) or green goddess dressing.

Ingredient tip: Substitute an equal amount of cooked rice for the quinoa.

SPICY TOMATO CHILI

SERVES 4 | PREP TIME: 15 MINUTES | COOK TIME: 1 HOUR 15 MINUTES

GLUTEN-FREE | NUT-FREE | ONE POT/PAN

This hearty and comforting chili is just the thing for a filling weeknight meal. Made with simple ingredients that are simmered together for bold flavor, this meal is sure to impress the entire family. Serve with corn chips or a side of homemade Southern Corn Bread (page 116).

1 tablespoon canola oil

1 onion, chopped

½ green bell pepper, seeded and chopped

2 garlic cloves, minced

1 (15-ounce) can pinto beans, drained and rinsed

1 (15-ounce) can kidney beans, drained and rinsed

2 (14.5-ounce) cans diced tomatoes, undrained

2 (4-ounce) cans diced green chilies

1 (8-ounce) can tomato sauce

1½ tablespoons chili powder

1½ teaspoons ground cumin

1 teaspoon dried oregano

1 teaspoon kosher salt

Shredded Cheddar cheese, for topping (optional)

Sour cream, for topping (optional)

Chips, for topping (optional)

Sliced scallions, for topping (optional)

1. In a Dutch oven or large stockpot, heat the oil over medium heat. Add the onion and bell pepper and cook for 3 to 5 minutes, or until the vegetables are slightly softened. Add the garlic and cook for about 1 minute, until fragrant.

2. Stir in the pinto beans, kidney beans, tomatoes and their juices, green chilies, tomato sauce, chili powder, cumin, oregano, and salt. Bring the chili to a simmer and cook over low heat for 1 hour, uncovered.

3. Serve topped with cheese, sour cream, chips, or scallions, as desired.

Addition tip: If you're not serving vegetarians, add 1 pound ground beef along with the onion and bell pepper. Cook for 5 minutes, or until the beef is crumbled and browned.

MUSHROOM STROGANOFF

SERVES 4 | PREP TIME: 20 MINUTES | COOK TIME: 4 HOURS

NUT-FREE | SLOW COOKER

This mushroom stroganoff slow cooks to perfection. My recipe uses cremini mushrooms, but you can use your favorite variety, as desired. Top this rich stroganoff with a dollop of cream cheese for a creamy, flavorful addition.

2 tablespoons unsalted butter

1 small onion, diced

2 garlic cloves, minced

2 cups sliced cremini mushrooms

2 tablespoons all-purpose flour

1 cup vegetable broth

1 teaspoon Dijon mustard

½ teaspoon dried thyme

½ teaspoon kosher salt

½ cup sour cream

8 ounces egg noodles, cooked

Chopped fresh parsley, for garnish

Cream cheese, for garnish

1. In a 10-inch skillet, melt the butter over medium heat. Add the onion and cook for 3 to 5 minutes, until soft. Add the garlic, mushrooms, and flour, stirring until no white remains. Transfer the onion mixture to a 4-quart slow cooker.

2. Add the vegetable broth, mustard, thyme, and salt.

3. Cover and cook on Low heat for 4 hours, stirring occasionally to avoid burning.

4. One hour before serving, stir the sour cream into the stroganoff.

5. Serve over cooked egg noodles with a sprinkle of parsley and a dollop of cream cheese.

Cooking tip: If you're using a slow cooker that's larger than 4 quarts, you may need to shorten the cook time or stir occasionally while cooking to avoid burning.

CREAMY TWO-CHEESE MACARONI

SERVES 4 | PREP TIME: 15 MINUTES | COOK TIME: 3 HOURS

NUT-FREE | SLOW COOKER

Classic slow cooker macaroni and cheese is one of my favorite family dinners. I like to whip this up for busy weeknights, or when we are in need of pure, simple comfort food.

Nonstick cooking spray

8 ounces elbow macaroni

1¼ cups whole milk

¾ cup evaporated milk

1½ cups shredded sharp Cheddar cheese

½ cup shredded pepper Jack cheese

½ teaspoon kosher salt

½ teaspoon dry mustard

¼ teaspoon freshly ground black pepper

¼ teaspoon garlic powder

3 tablespoons unsalted butter

1. Mist a 4-quart slow cooker with cooking spray.

2. In the prepared cooker, combine the macaroni, whole milk, evaporated milk, Cheddar cheese, Jack cheese, salt, mustard, pepper, and garlic powder. Stir to combine.

3. Dot the top with the butter, cover, and cook on Low heat for 2 to 3 hours, stirring once at the halfway mark, if possible, to avoid burning, until the pasta is cooked through.

Ingredient tip: Always buy block cheese and shred the amount you need. Preshredded cheeses include additives that make the finished dish less smooth and creamy.

Addition tip: One hour before serving, toss in a handful of diced broccoli for a veggie-enhanced dish.

BLACK BEAN TACO-STUFFED PEPPERS

SERVES 4 | PREP TIME: 10 MINUTES | COOK TIME: 3 TO 6 HOURS

GLUTEN-FREE | NUT-FREE | SLOW COOKER

These filling and flavor-packed stuffed peppers take taco Tuesday to an entirely new level! The filling is delicious all on its own, but it becomes something really special when cooked slowly inside a bell pepper. This recipe calls for cooked rice, but cooked quinoa would be a good substitute.

1 (15-ounce) can black beans, drained and rinsed

1 cup corn kernels

1 cup cooked rice

½ cup salsa

½ cup enchilada sauce

2 tablespoons Taco Seasoning (page 156) or store-bought seasoning

1 cup shredded pepper Jack cheese, divided

4 large bell peppers, any color, tops cut off, seeded and ribbed

½ cup water

1. In a medium bowl, stir together the black beans, corn, cooked rice, salsa, enchilada sauce, taco seasoning, and ½ cup of Jack cheese. Evenly divide the filling among the cleaned peppers.

2. Stand the peppers in a 4-quart slow cooker. You may have to trim off a small piece from the bottoms of the peppers for them to stand upright. Pour the water around the peppers into the slow cooker.

3. Cover and cook on High heat for 3 hours, or on Low heat for 6 hours, or until the peppers are tender.

4. During the last few minutes of cooking, top each pepper with 2 tablespoons of the remaining cheese. Serve when the cheese has melted.

Cooking tip: If you're using a slow cooker that's larger than 4 quarts, you may need to shorten the cook time or stir occasionally while cooking.

Ingredient tip: I like to use green salsa for this recipe, but red salsa works well, too.

GARLIC PARMESAN PASTA

SERVES 4 | PREP TIME: 10 MINUTES | COOK TIME: 20 MINUTES

30-MINUTE | NUT-FREE | ONE POT/PAN

If I had to pick my favorite one-pot recipe from this book, it would be this one. The pasta is cooked with fresh garlic and basil, which add a boost in flavor you would not expect. Did I mention it is also incredibly simple to make? Everything is tossed into one pot and the result is a creamy tomato sauce that is difficult to resist. Substitute ¼ cup pesto for the basil, or top with 1 pound cooked sausage or chicken for extra protein if you are feeding meat-eaters.

12 ounces rotini pasta

2 cups vegetable broth

1¾ cups water

1 onion, quartered

½ cup fresh basil leaves

3 garlic cloves, minced

3 ounces cream cheese

1½ cups jarred pasta sauce

¼ cup freshly shredded Parmesan cheese

1. In a large Dutch oven or pot, combine the pasta, vegetable broth, water, onion, and basil. Bring to a boil over medium-high heat. Reduce the heat to low and simmer for about 10 minutes, or until most of the liquid is gone and the pasta is almost al dente.

2. Stir in the cream cheese, mixing until it's completely melted, followed by the pasta sauce and Parmesan cheese. Cook for 2 to 3 minutes to warm. Serve immediately.

Ingredient tip: The pasta sauce and fresh basil are the biggest sources of flavor here, so use a high-quality sauce and the freshest basil for best results.

PERSONAL MARGHERITA PIZZAS

SERVES 4 | PREP TIME: 10 MINUTES | COOK TIME: 10 MINUTES

5-INGREDIENT | 30-MINUTE | NUT-FREE

These personal flatbread pizzas come together in a flash for a fun dinner the whole family can make together. You can use store-bought pizza sauce, but to kick things to the next level, use my garlic and herb pizza sauce.

4 store-bought flatbreads

½ cup Garlic and Herb Pizza Sauce (page 151) or store-bought pizza sauce

¾ cup cubed (½-inch) fresh mozzarella cheese

¼ cup grated Parmesan cheese

¼ cup fresh basil leaves

1. Preheat the oven to 425°F.

2. Place the flatbreads on a sheet pan. Spread 2 tablespoons of pizza sauce over each.

3. Dot each flatbread with mozzarella cheese and sprinkle with Parmesan cheese.

4. Bake for 8 to 10 minutes, or until the cheese is melted. Top with fresh basil and serve.

Addition tip: Do not be afraid to add your favorite toppings to this pizza. My family loves pepperoni, garlic Alfredo sauce, red onion, bell pepper, and mushrooms!

BROCCOLI LO MEIN

SERVES 4 | PREP TIME: 15 MINUTES | COOK TIME: 15 MINUTES
30-MINUTE | DAIRY-FREE | NUT-FREE

Forget takeout! This kid-approved broccoli lo mein comes together in 30 minutes and features loads of veggies.

6 ounces Chinese egg noodles

2 tablespoons light brown sugar

2 tablespoons soy sauce

1 tablespoon rice vinegar

2 teaspoons minced garlic

2 teaspoons cornstarch

¼ teaspoon sesame oil

¼ teaspoon Chinese five-spice powder

¼ teaspoon ground ginger, or 1 teaspoon grated peeled fresh ginger

½ teaspoon sriracha

2 teaspoons extra-virgin olive oil

3 cups prepackaged broccoli slaw or shredded veggies of choice, like Brussels sprouts or cabbage

¼ cup sliced scallions

1. Cook the egg noodles according to the package directions. Drain and set aside.

2. In a small saucepan, stir together the brown sugar, soy sauce, rice vinegar, garlic, cornstarch, sesame oil, five-spice powder, ginger, and sriracha. Bring just to a boil over medium heat. Remove from the heat.

3. In a large skillet, heat the olive oil over medium heat. Toss in the broccoli slaw and sauté for 2 to 3 minutes, until the veggies are tender. Add the cooked noodles, sauce, and scallions. Toss to combine.

Addition tip: If there are no vegetarians at your table, add 2 large chopped cooked chicken breasts to the lo mein.

EASY FETTUCCINE ALFREDO

SERVES 4 | PREP TIME: 10 MINUTES | COOK TIME: 20 MINUTES
5-INGREDIENT | 30-MINUTE | NUT-FREE

Anything that can come together in 30 minutes with only 5 ingredients is a lifesaver, especially on busy weeknights! This Alfredo is great when you need a break from traditional red sauce. Use fresh, not preshredded, Parmigiano-Reggiano cheese for a smooth sauce.

8 ounces fettuccine

4 tablespoons (½ stick) salted butter

2 garlic cloves, minced

1 cup heavy (whipping) cream

1½ cups shredded Parmigiano-Reggiano cheese

Chopped fresh parsley, for garnish (optional)

1. Cook the pasta according to the package directions. Drain and set aside.

2. In a medium stockpot, melt the butter over medium heat. Stir in the garlic and cook for 1 minute.

3. Whisk the heavy cream into the garlic butter. Bring the sauce to a simmer and cook for 5 minutes, stirring constantly.

4. Add the Parmesan cheese and stir until melted.

5. Add the cooked pasta and toss with the sauce. Serve garnished with fresh parsley (if using).

Addition tip: Add 1 cup sliced mushrooms and a sprinkle of parsley to the sauce for a flavor twist.

SPINACH AND CHEESE RAVIOLI BAKE

SERVES 4 | PREP TIME: 20 MINUTES | COOK TIME: 1 HOUR

5-INGREDIENT | MAKE AHEAD | NUT-FREE

This recipe is the definition of easy. All you need is a bag of frozen cheese ravioli, your favorite pasta sauce, and some frozen spinach for a filling meal. Assemble this up to 24 hours in advance for a super-quick meal that can be put into the oven and ready to eat in about 1 hour.

Nonstick cooking spray

2½ cups jarred pasta sauce, divided

½ cup frozen chopped spinach, thawed and drained

1 (25-ounce) bag frozen cheese ravioli

2 cups shredded Italian cheese blend

1. Preheat the oven to 350°F. Mist a 13-by-9-inch baking pan with cooking spray.

2. In a small bowl, stir together 1 cup of pasta sauce and the spinach. Set aside.

3. Spread about ½ cup of pasta sauce over the bottom of the prepared pan.

4. Arrange a single layer of ravioli over the sauce. This should use about one-third of the package.

5. Spread the spinach mixture over the ravioli. Top with another layer of ravioli.

6. Cover the ravioli with ½ cup of pasta sauce and sprinkle with 1 cup of cheese. Repeat this layer (ravioli, sauce, cheese). Cover the baking dish with aluminum foil.

7. Bake for 40 minutes. Remove the foil and bake for 20 minutes more, or until the cheese is melted and the sauce is bubbling.

Addition tip: For nonvegetarian friends, add 1 pound cooked sausage to the spinach mixture.

Make ahead tip: To freeze, complete the recipe through step 6 and let cool slightly. Place the covered pan in a freezer-safe bag or cover it with aluminum foil and freeze for up to 3 months. When ready to cook, bake according to the recipe instructions, adding 15 minutes to the baking time.

SOUTHWEST STUFFED
SWEET POTATOES

SERVES 4 | PREP TIME: 10 MINUTES | COOK TIME: 6 TO 8 HOURS

DAIRY-FREE | GLUTEN-FREE | NUT-FREE | SLOW COOKER

These delectable sweet potatoes cook slowly all day, filling your house with a mouthwatering aroma. Chop the onion and bell pepper in advance and store them in the freezer for super-quick prep. No sweet potatoes? This recipe also works great with russet potatoes.

4 large sweet potatoes

1 tablespoon canola oil

½ onion, chopped

½ red bell pepper, seeded and chopped

1 cup canned black beans, drained and rinsed

2 tablespoons water

2 teaspoons Taco Seasoning (page 156) or store-bought taco seasoning

Homemade Guacamole (page 123), for serving

Pico de gallo, for serving

1. Scrub the potatoes clean and dry them thoroughly. Prick each potato with a fork 4 or 5 times. Place the potatoes in a 4-quart slow cooker.

2. Cover and cook on Low heat for 6 to 8 hours, or until soft.

3. Ten minutes before serving, in a 10-inch skillet, heat the oil over medium heat. Add the onion and red bell pepper and cook for 5 minutes, or until the bell pepper is tender. Stir in the black beans, water, and seasoning. Simmer for 5 minutes, or until heated through.

4. Carefully remove the potatoes from the slow cooker. Split each potato open lengthwise and divide the bean filling among them. Serve with guacamole and pico de gallo.

Cooking tip: If you're using a slow cooker that's larger than 4 quarts, you may need to shorten the cook time.

BLACK BEAN BURGERS

SERVES 4 | PREP TIME: 10 MINUTES | COOK TIME: 20 MINUTES
30-MINUTE | DAIRY-FREE | MAKE AHEAD | NUT-FREE

I love burgers. In fact, my entire family loves burgers. Grilling season is our jam, and although we are mainly red meat eaters, these baked black bean burgers have planted their spot firmly in our top two summer must-makes. They are also perfect to make in advance and freeze for a quick dinner.

Nonstick cooking spray

1 (15-ounce) can black beans, drained and rinsed

½ red bell pepper, seeded and cut into ½-inch chunks

½ onion, cut into ½-inch chunks

3 garlic cloves, peeled

2 large egg yolks

1 tablespoon chili powder

1 teaspoon ground cumin

1 teaspoon hot sauce

1 cup quick-cooking oats, Homemade Bread Crumbs (page 158), or store-bought bread crumbs

1. Preheat the oven to 375°F. Line a sheet pan with aluminum foil and mist it with cooking spray. Set aside.

2. Pat the black beans dry with a paper towel and transfer to a small bowl. Using a fork, roughly mash the beans. Set aside.

3. In a blender or food processor, combine the red bell pepper, onion, and garlic. Pulse until finely chopped. Drain off any excess liquid and stir the vegetables into the black beans.

4. In another small bowl, stir together the egg yolks, chili powder, cumin, and hot sauce. Add the seasoned eggs to the black bean mixture and stir to combine. Stir in the oats. Divide the mixture into 4 portions and shape each into a patty about ½ inch thick. Place the patties on the prepared baking sheet.

5. Bake for 10 minutes, flip, and bake until they reach an internal temperature of 165°F, about 10 minutes more.

6. Serve as desired. We like ours on buns with chipotle mayo, tomato slices, and avocado slices.

Make ahead tip: To freeze, place the assembled, uncooked burgers on a tray and freeze for 20 minutes. Then individually wrap each frozen patty in plastic wrap and place in a freezer-safe zip-top bag. Freeze for up to 3 months. Remove from the freezer and thaw in the refrigerator at least 4 hours before cooking as instructed.

ORANGE CAULIFLOWER BOWLS

SERVES 4 | PREP TIME: 20 MINUTES | COOK TIME: 20 MINUTES
DAIRY-FREE

My 11-year-old has no idea this is cauliflower—and loves it anyway—which I consider a serious parenting win. You can also try this delicious sauce over chopped cooked chicken for a meaty variation!

2 cups Homemade Bread Crumbs (page 158) or store-bought bread crumbs

1 cup water

¾ cup all-purpose flour

1 tablespoon garlic powder, plus ¼ teaspoon

¼ teaspoon kosher salt

5 cups cauliflower florets, cut into bite-size pieces

1 cup freshly squeezed orange juice

½ cup sugar

2 tablespoons rice vinegar

2 tablespoons soy sauce

½ teaspoon red pepper flakes

¼ teaspoon minced peeled fresh ginger

1 tablespoon cornstarch

Grated zest of 1 orange

1 cup basmati rice, cooked according to the package directions

1. Preheat the oven to 400°F. Line a sheet pan with parchment paper. Set aside.
2. Place the bread crumbs in a shallow dish.
3. In a large bowl, whisk together the water, flour, 1 tablespoon of garlic powder, and salt.
4. Working in batches, dip the cauliflower florets into the batter, allowing any excess to drip off. Roll them in the bread crumbs. Place on the prepared baking sheet, making sure the pieces do not touch to ensure even browning.
5. Bake for 20 minutes, or until golden brown and crisp.
6. While the cauliflower bakes, in a medium pot, combine the orange juice, sugar, rice vinegar, soy sauce, red pepper flakes, ginger, and remaining ¼ teaspoon of garlic powder. Bring to a simmer over medium heat and cook for about 3 minutes.
7. In a small bowl, whisk the cornstarch with 2 tablespoons of the orange juice mixture to form a paste. Whisk the paste into the rest of the orange juice mixture and simmer for 5 minutes, or until the mixture begins to thicken. Stir in the orange zest. Transfer the sauce to a medium bowl.
8. Add the baked cauliflower to the sauce and toss to coat. Serve over cooked rice.

Ingredient tip: Purchase precut cauliflower to reduce prep time.

CRISPY BAKED QUESADILLAS

SERVES 4 | PREP TIME: 10 MINUTES | COOK TIME: 20 MINUTES
30-MINUTE | MAKE AHEAD | NUT-FREE | ONE POT/PAN

Quesadillas are great because you can use up any ingredients on the verge of spoiling. We like to bake ours for a nice crispy outside and fill them with any vegetables we have on hand. I suggest corn and bell pepper to get you started, but don't hesitate to get creative.

1 (15-ounce) can black beans, drained and rinsed

1 cup corn

1 red or green bell pepper, seeded and chopped

⅓ cup salsa

2½ cups shredded Cheddar cheese

4 (10-inch) flour tortillas

Pico de gallo, for serving (optional)

Homemade Guacamole (page 123), for serving (optional)

Sour cream, for serving (optional)

1. Preheat the oven to 350°F. Line a sheet pan with parchment paper. Set aside.

2. In a medium bowl, stir together the black beans, corn, red bell pepper, salsa, and Cheddar cheese.

3. Place the tortillas on the prepared baking sheet. Divide the filling among the tortillas, spooning it onto one side of each. Fold the other side of the tortillas over the filling.

4. Bake for 20 minutes, or until the tortillas are slightly crispy.

Make ahead tip: Quesadillas can be frozen before they are baked. To freeze, follow the recipe through step 3. Tightly wrap each quesadilla in plastic wrap and place in a freezer-safe zip-top bag or container. Freeze for up to 3 months. When ready to eat, bake directly from frozen at 350°F for 30 minutes.

HOMEMADE PESTO PASTA

SERVES 4 | PREP TIME: 20 MINUTES

5-INGREDIENT | 30-MINUTE | DAIRY-FREE | MAKE AHEAD

Pesto can add so much flavor to a dish with only a handful of easy ingredients. Serve it over pasta as I do here, on chicken, vegetables, or pizza, or mix into dips for a flavor boost! The pesto here is a thinner coating sauce; if you want it thicker for dipping, use half the oil.

2 cups fresh basil leaves

2 tablespoons toasted pine nuts

2 garlic cloves, peeled

1 tablespoon freshly squeezed lemon juice

½ cup extra-virgin olive oil

½ teaspoon sea salt (optional)

2 cups freshly cooked pasta

1. In a high-powered blender or food processor, combine the basil, pine nuts, garlic, and lemon juice. Pulse until finely minced.

2. With the blender running, drizzle the oil into the mixture and process until smooth. Season with salt (if using).

3. Transfer the sauce to a medium bowl, add the pasta, and toss to combine.

Addition tip: Stir in ½ cup grated Parmesan cheese or sprinkle some red pepper flakes on top before serving for even more flavor.

Storage tip: Refrigerate the pesto in an airtight container for up to 5 days or freeze for up to 6 months.

GREEN CHILE CHEESE ENCHILADAS

SERVES 4 | PREP TIME: 10 MINUTES | COOK TIME: 2 TO 4 HOURS

NUT-FREE | SLOW COOKER

This is the recipe I keep on the back burner for those nights when I just do not want to spend time in the kitchen. I keep these enchiladas simple, with just a cheese filling, but you can add ½ cup each of cooked bell pepper, mushroom, and onion.

Nonstick cooking spray

2 cups enchilada sauce, divided

8 (8-inch) flour tortillas

1½ cups shredded Mexican cheese blend, divided

1 (4-ounce) can diced green chiles

Shredded lettuce, for serving

Diced tomato, for serving

Sour cream, for serving

1. Mist a 4-quart slow cooker with cooking spray. Spread 1 cup of enchilada sauce on the bottom of the prepared cooker.

2. Place the tortillas on a clean work surface. Cover each tortilla with 2 tablespoons of shredded cheese and ½ ounce chiles and roll up. Place the tortillas, seam-side down, in the slow cooker. If using a smaller slow cooker, stack the enchiladas in two layers.

3. Pour the remaining enchilada sauce over the filled tortillas. Sprinkle the top with the remaining ½ cup of cheese.

4. Cover and cook on High heat for 2 hours, or on Low heat for 4 hours.

5. Serve with lettuce, tomato, sour cream, and any other toppings you like.

Cooking tip: To make these in the oven, prepare in a 13-by-9-inch baking pan and bake at 400°F for 20 minutes.

HUMMUS, OLIVE, AND TOMATO FLATBREAD

SERVES 4 | PREP TIME: 15 MINUTES | COOK TIME: 5 MINUTES
30-MINUTE | NUT-FREE

Flatbread is versatile and delicious. This Greek-style flatbread recipe combines hummus, tomato, and artichoke for a wonderful meal that's ready in about 20 minutes. If you do not have flatbread, naan also works well.

1 cup artichoke hearts, drained, rinsed, and chopped

1 cup cherry tomatoes, halved

½ cup Greek olives, pitted and sliced

¼ cup fresh parsley, chopped

1 tablespoon extra-virgin olive oil

Kosher salt

Freshly ground black pepper

4 store-bought flatbreads

½ cup hummus

Feta cheese, for garnish

1. Preheat the oven to 400°F. Line a sheet pan with parchment paper. Set aside.

2. In a medium bowl, toss together the artichoke hearts, tomatoes, olives, parsley, and oil. Season with salt and pepper to taste.

3. Place the flatbreads on a clean work surface and spread 2 tablespoons of hummus onto each. Divide the vegetable filling among the flatbreads.

4. Bake for 5 minutes, or until warm. Top with feta cheese and serve.

BUILD-YOUR-OWN BUDDHA BOWL

SERVES 4 | PREP TIME: 10 MINUTES | COOK TIME: 20 MINUTES
30-MINUTE | DAIRY-FREE | GLUTEN-FREE | MAKE AHEAD | ONE POT/PAN

I love this recipe for so many reasons. The top three? It is simple to make, comes together quickly, and is ideal for meal prep. I use canned chickpeas, but you could also use dried chickpeas that have been soaked in water overnight, drained, and cooked.

1 (15-ounce) can chickpeas, drained and rinsed

2 cups broccoli florets

1 cup chopped carrot

1 tablespoon vegetable oil

Kosher salt

Freshly ground black pepper

2 cups cooked quinoa

¼ cup peanut sauce (optional)

1. Preheat the oven to 400°F. Line a sheet pan with parchment paper or aluminum foil.

2. Spread the chickpeas, broccoli, and carrot on the prepared baking sheet. Drizzle with the oil and season with salt and pepper. Gently stir to coat.

3. Bake for 10 minutes, stir, and bake for 10 minutes more until the chickpeas and vegetables are slightly crisp.

4. Divide the quinoa into 4 bowls and top with the chickpea mixture.

5. Serve with peanut sauce for drizzling (if using).

Variation tip: No broccoli? No problem! This recipe works well with most vegetables, so use whatever you have on hand.

POULTRY AND SEAFOOD MAINS

< Sheet Pan Lemon Chicken and Potatoes, p. 79

COMFORTING CHICKEN POTPIE

SERVES 8 | PREP TIME: 15 MINUTES | COOK TIME: 40 MINUTES

MAKE AHEAD | NUT-FREE

This semi-homemade chicken potpie comes together quickly and can be made ahead and frozen. A classic comfort food, this version uses frozen vegetable blends and cream of chicken soup to create an easy weeknight dinner. Thyme is my favorite herb to use here. However, you could substitute an equal amount of Italian Seasoning (page 156) for a change.

2 store-bought refrigerated deep-dish piecrusts

1½ cups cubed or shredded rotisserie chicken

1 (10.75-ounce) can cream of chicken soup

¼ cup chicken broth

1⅔ cups frozen mixed vegetables, thawed

½ teaspoon dried thyme

½ teaspoon onion powder

¼ teaspoon freshly ground black pepper

1. Preheat the oven to 400°F.
2. Unroll one piecrust into a deep 9-inch pie dish. Set aside.
3. In a large bowl, combine the chicken, cream of chicken soup, chicken broth, mixed vegetables, thyme, onion powder, and pepper. Mix well and transfer to the prepared piecrust.
4. Gently lay the second crust on top of the potpie. Trim and crimp the edges. Cut 3 slits in the top with a knife to let steam escape.
5. Bake for 35 to 40 minutes, or until the crust is lightly browned. Let stand for 15 minutes before cutting and serving.

Make ahead tip: The potpie filling can be made and kept refrigerated up to 1 day in advance. To freeze the potpie to eat later, follow the recipe through step 4. Tightly cover the potpie with plastic wrap and place it in a freezer-safe zip-top bag. Freeze for up to 2 months. Bake for 50 to 65 minutes in a 400°F oven. Cover the potpie with aluminum foil halfway through the baking time and bake until the crust is lightly browned.

BROCCOLI AND CHICKEN STIR-FRY

SERVES 4 | PREP TIME: 15 MINUTES | COOK TIME: 25 MINUTES

DAIRY-FREE | NUT-FREE | ONE POT/PAN

This stir-fry is the perfect one-pot meal! Everything comes together quickly and this dish is packed with veggies, making it a delicious and healthy addition to your meal rotation. It is very versatile and easy to customize by adding different vegetables. Consider shaking things up with zucchini, yellow squash, or onion.

3 tablespoons vegetable oil, divided

1 pound boneless, skinless chicken breasts, cubed

Kosher salt

Freshly ground black pepper

2 cups broccoli florets

1 cup sliced mushrooms

1 cup sliced red bell pepper

½ cup thinly sliced carrot

1 cup chicken broth

⅓ cup lower-sodium soy sauce

2 tablespoons cornstarch

1 tablespoon light brown sugar

2 garlic cloves, minced

2 teaspoons sesame oil

½ to 1 teaspoon minced peeled fresh ginger

Cooked rice, for serving (optional)

¼ cup sliced scallions (optional)

1 tablespoon sesame seeds (optional)

1. In a large pan or wok, heat 1 tablespoon of vegetable oil over medium heat.

2. Season the chicken all over with salt and pepper. Add to the pan and cook for about 10 minutes, until the chicken is cooked through and no longer pink. Transfer the chicken to a plate and cover to keep warm.

3. Return the pan to the heat and add the remaining 2 tablespoons of vegetable oil. Add the broccoli, mushrooms, red bell pepper, and carrot and cook for 3 to 5 minutes, stirring frequently, until the vegetables begin to soften.

4. Stir in the chicken broth, soy sauce, cornstarch, brown sugar, garlic, sesame oil, and ginger to combine. Return the chicken to the pan and cook for 5 to 7 minutes, or until the sauce has slightly thickened. Serve over rice, if desired, sprinkled with scallions (if using) and sesame seeds (if using).

GO-TO GRILLED CHICKEN

SERVES 4 | PREP TIME: 10 MINUTES, PLUS 4 HOURS TO MARINATE | COOK TIME: 10 MINUTES

DAIRY-FREE | GLUTEN-FREE | MAKE AHEAD | NUT-FREE

Everyone should have one quality chicken recipe up their sleeve. This marinade is incredibly simple and delicious. I make a large batch of this grilled chicken and keep it in the freezer. Whenever I need grilled chicken for a recipe, like my Baked Chicken Quesadillas (page 76), it is ready to go! This chicken is also great on its own, served with a simple side salad or Garlic Mushroom Fried Rice (page 48).

¼ cup packed light brown sugar

3 tablespoons extra-virgin olive oil

2 tablespoons apple cider vinegar

2 tablespoons freshly squeezed lemon juice

1½ tablespoons Dijon mustard

2 garlic cloves, minced

1 teaspoon kosher salt

¼ teaspoon freshly ground black pepper

1 pound boneless, skinless chicken breasts, pounded ¼ inch thick or halved horizontally into cutlets

1. In a small bowl, whisk the brown sugar, oil, vinegar, lemon juice, mustard, garlic, salt, and pepper until combined. Transfer the marinade to a large zip-top bag or airtight container and add the chicken, turning once to coat. Refrigerate for at least 4 hours, or up to 24 hours.

2. Preheat a grill or grill pan to medium heat. Close the lid and let the grill warm for 15 minutes.

3. Remove the chicken from the marinade and place it on the grill. Discard the marinade. Cook for 2 to 3 minutes per side, or until the chicken reaches an internal temperature of 165°F. Remove from the heat, slice, and use in your favorite recipes.

Cooking tip: You can make this chicken in the oven. Preheat the broiler. Place the marinated chicken on a sheet pan and broil for 2 to 3 minutes per side until the chicken reaches an internal temperature of 165°F.

Make ahead tip: Once cooked, you can freeze the chicken pieces (whole or sliced) in a freezer-safe zip-top bag for up to 4 months. Remove from the freezer and reheat on the stovetop over medium heat for about 8 minutes.

CRISPY DIJON BAKED CHICKEN

SERVES 4 | PREP TIME: 10 MINUTES | COOK TIME: 30 MINUTES

5-INGREDIENT | NUT-FREE

My 11-year-old son insists that if you only make one recipe from this section, this should be the one. We have been making this easy baked chicken for years and it never disappoints. Chicken breasts are dipped in a mixture of butter and Dijon mustard, rolled in bread crumbs and Parmesan, and baked to crispy perfection!

Nonstick cooking spray

4 tablespoons (½ stick) salted butter, melted

2 tablespoons Dijon mustard

¾ cup Italian-style bread crumbs (see Homemade Bread Crumbs, page 158) or store-bought

¼ cup grated Parmesan cheese

2 large boneless, skinless chicken breasts, halved horizontally into cutlets

1. Preheat the oven to 425°F. Mist a 9-by-13-inch baking dish with cooking spray. Set aside.

2. In a shallow bowl, whisk the melted butter and mustard to combine. Set aside.

3. In another shallow bowl, stir together the bread crumbs and Parmesan cheese. Set aside.

4. Dip each piece of chicken in the mustard-butter, then into the bread crumbs, coating well on both sides. Place the coated chicken in a single layer in the prepared baking dish.

5. Bake for 20 to 30 minutes, or until the internal temperature of the chicken reaches 165°F.

Variation tip: Although I often use this chicken in other recipes, it's also amazing when served as is, with roasted veggies (see Easy Roasted Vegetables, page 114) on the side.

PEANUT-GINGER TURKEY LETTUCE WRAPS

SERVES 4 | PREP TIME: 15 MINUTES | COOK TIME: 15 MINUTES
30-MINUTE | DAIRY-FREE

These lettuce wraps are fantastic for your friends who are on low-carb diets or anyone looking for an out-of-the-box ground turkey recipe. I like to use Boston Bibb lettuce or romaine hearts, but any leafy green will do.

¼ cup lower-sodium soy sauce

1 tablespoon sugar

2 teaspoons sesame oil

1 teaspoon peanut sauce

1 pound ground turkey

2 teaspoons minced peeled fresh ginger

1 garlic clove, minced

1 cup canned water chestnuts, drained and chopped

½ red bell pepper, seeded and chopped

¼ cup shredded carrot

2 cups cooked rice

8 large lettuce leaves

1. In a small bowl, whisk the soy sauce, sugar, sesame oil, and peanut sauce to combine. Set aside.

2. Heat a 10-inch skillet over medium heat. Add the turkey and cook for about 10 minutes, until crumbled and browned.

3. Stir in the ginger and garlic and cook for 1 minute more.

4. Stir in the soy sauce mixture, water chestnuts, red bell pepper, and carrot. Cook for 3 minutes.

5. Remove the skillet from the heat and stir in the cooked rice.

6. Spoon heaping tablespoons of the filling onto the lettuce leaves and enjoy.

Cooking tip: The vegetables in this wrap are intentionally crunchy; if you prefer softer vegetables, add them when you begin cooking the turkey.

SHEET PAN CHICKEN FAJITAS

SERVES 4 | PREP TIME: 15 MINUTES | COOK TIME: 20 MINUTES

DAIRY-FREE | NUT-FREE | ONE POT/PAN

Keep fajitas simple with this delicious sheet pan option. Toss the chicken and veggies on the pan and bake—then revel in the quick cleanup!

Nonstick cooking spray (optional)

2 large boneless, skinless chicken breasts, cut into ½-inch-thick strips

1 yellow onion, sliced

1 green bell pepper, seeded and sliced

1 red bell pepper, seeded and sliced

3 garlic cloves, minced

3 tablespoons extra-virgin olive oil

3 tablespoons Fajita Seasoning (page 156) or store-bought seasoning

2 limes, halved

8 (6-inch) corn or flour tortillas, warmed

1. Preheat the oven to 400°F. Mist a large sheet pan with cooking spray or line it with aluminum foil for easy cleanup.

2. Spread the chicken, onion, green bell pepper, red bell pepper, and garlic on the prepared pan. Drizzle with the olive oil and fajita seasoning. Toss to coat evenly.

3. Bake for 10 minutes, stir, and bake for 10 minutes more, or until the chicken reaches an internal temperature of 165°F.

4. Squeeze lime juice over the fajita mixture and serve in warmed tortillas with your toppings of choice (see Addition tip below).

Addition tip: I recommend topping your fajitas with sour cream, Homemade Guacamole (page 123), and fresh cilantro.

BAKED CHICKEN QUESADILLAS

SERVES 4 | PREP TIME: 10 MINUTES | COOK TIME: 16 MINUTES
5-INGREDIENT | 30-MINUTE | NUT-FREE

These baked quesadillas are incredibly easy to make. Cooked chicken is tossed with shredded cheese, salsa, and sour cream for a quick, filling meal. Bake until you get a perfectly crispy tortilla.

Nonstick cooking spray

1½ cups shredded Cheddar cheese

1 cup shredded or diced cooked chicken

3 tablespoons green salsa

1 tablespoon sour cream

4 (8-inch) flour tortillas

1. Preheat the oven to 425°F. Mist a sheet pan with cooking spray. Set aside.
2. In a medium bowl, stir together the Cheddar cheese, chicken, salsa, and sour cream. Divide the filling among the tortillas, keeping it all on one side to allow for folding. Fold the other side of the tortillas over the filling and place them on the prepared baking sheet.
3. Mist the top of the quesadillas with cooking spray. Bake for 8 minutes, flip (no need to spray again), and bake for 8 minutes more, until the tortillas are slightly browned and crisp.

Cooking tip: My Go-To Grilled Chicken (page 72) would be perfect in this dish.

GARLIC CHICKEN WITH CARROTS AND POTATOES

SERVES 4 | PREP TIME: 5 MINUTES | COOK TIME: 5 HOURS

DAIRY-FREE | GLUTEN-FREE | NUT-FREE | SLOW COOKER

Garlic lovers rejoice! This chicken recipe is incredibly delicious, and the addition of carrots and potatoes makes a full meal. Remember that low and slow is the key to this dish. Keep it on the Low setting for about 4 hours and you will get juicy, perfectly cooked chicken!

2 large potatoes, cut into 1-inch cubes

1 cup whole baby carrots

1 large yellow onion, chopped

6 garlic cloves, minced

½ cup chicken broth

1 pound boneless, skinless chicken breasts or thighs

1½ teaspoons dried thyme

1 teaspoon dried basil

1 teaspoon dried oregano

½ teaspoon kosher salt

1. In a 4-quart slow cooker, combine the potatoes, carrots, onion, and garlic. Pour the chicken broth over the vegetables and arrange the chicken on top.

2. In a small bowl, stir together the thyme, basil, oregano, and salt. Sprinkle the herbs over the chicken and vegetables.

3. Cover and cook on Low heat for 4 to 5 hours, or until the chicken reaches an internal temperature of 165°F and the vegetables are tender.

Cooking tip: This recipe produces just enough liquid to make a quick chicken gravy. Whisk the leftover liquid with your favorite gravy packet. If you're using a slow cooker that's larger than 4 quarts, you may need to shorten the cook time or stir occasionally while cooking.

Ingredient tip: You can use bottled minced garlic, but the best results come with using fresh garlic.

ROSEMARY AND THYME TURKEY BREAST

SERVES 4 OR 5 | PREP TIME: 10 MINUTES | COOK TIME: 6 HOURS

DAIRY-FREE | GLUTEN-FREE | NUT-FREE | SLOW COOKER

Turkey is not just for Thanksgiving. As a small family of three, we like to reach for a turkey breast instead of the entire bird. It is small enough to feed our family without a month of leftovers. Brushed with olive oil and sprinkled with herbs, this turkey is slow-roasted in the slow cooker and gives you a moist and juicy bird.

1 (4- to 5-pound) bone-in turkey breast

1 tablespoon extra-virgin olive oil

2 garlic cloves, minced

1 teaspoon dry mustard

1 teaspoon kosher salt

½ teaspoon freshly ground black pepper

1½ teaspoons fresh rosemary leaves

1½ teaspoons chopped fresh sage

1½ teaspoons fresh thyme leaves

½ cup water

1. Brush the turkey breast with the oil and place it in a 4-quart slow cooker.

2. Sprinkle the garlic over the turkey followed by the mustard, salt, and pepper. Top with the rosemary, sage, and thyme.

3. Pour the water around the turkey into the slow cooker.

4. Cover and cook on Low heat for 6 hours, or until tender and the turkey reaches an internal temperature of 165°F.

Substitution tip: If you do not have fresh herbs on hand, substitute with ½ teaspoon dried rosemary, ½ teaspoon dried sage, and ½ teaspoon dried thyme instead.

SHEET PAN LEMON CHICKEN AND POTATOES

SERVES 4 | PREP TIME: 15 MINUTES | COOK TIME: 35 MINUTES

GLUTEN-FREE | NUT-FREE | ONE POT/PAN

Chicken thighs are a delicious part of the chicken. They are less expensive than breasts and just as simple to bake. In this recipe, I cover them with a delicious lemon-butter sauce. Combined with crisp golden potatoes and fresh green beans, you get a one-pan dinner that earns a four-star rating.

Nonstick cooking spray

4 tablespoons (½ stick) unsalted butter, melted

⅓ cup chicken broth

¼ cup freshly squeezed lemon juice

3 garlic cloves, minced

1 teaspoon Italian Seasoning (page 156) or store-bought seasoning

3 pounds boneless, skin-on chicken thighs (remove the skin, if you prefer)

1 pound Yukon Gold potatoes, peeled and cut into 1-inch pieces

1 teaspoon kosher salt

1 teaspoon freshly ground black pepper

8 ounces green beans, trimmed

1. Preheat the oven to 400°F. Mist a sheet pan with cooking spray. Set aside.

2. In a medium measuring cup, whisk the melted butter, chicken broth, lemon juice, garlic, and Italian seasoning to combine.

3. Place the chicken on the prepared pan. Arrange the potatoes around the chicken. Sprinkle with the salt and pepper. Drizzle half the prepared sauce over the chicken. Gently stir the ingredients on the pan to coat in the sauce.

4. Bake for 15 minutes. Remove from the oven and flip the chicken. Move the potatoes to one side of the pan and add the green beans to the other side. Pour the remaining sauce over the green beans and gently mix to coat.

5. Bake for 20 minutes more, or until the chicken reaches an internal temperature of 165°F.

SHEET PAN TILAPIA WITH ASPARAGUS

SERVES 4 | PREP TIME: 10 MINUTES | COOK TIME: 12 MINUTES

5-INGREDIENT | 30-MINUTE | GLUTEN-FREE | NUT-FREE | ONE POT/PAN

Tilapia is a great fish for new cooks and new fish-eaters alike. It has a mild flavor and pairs well with most flavor profiles. When cooking this fish, I like to brush it with an herbed butter sauce before baking. Prep time is minimal, and you can swap in almost any vegetable. We like asparagus, but you could easily use green beans or Brussels sprouts!

Nonstick cooking spray

1 pound asparagus, woody ends trimmed

1 tablespoon extra-virgin olive oil

Kosher salt

Freshly ground black pepper

2 tablespoons unsalted butter, melted

½ teaspoon garlic salt

½ teaspoon Italian Seasoning (page 156) or store-bought seasoning

4 tilapia fillets

1. Preheat the oven to 425°F. Mist a sheet pan with cooking spray.

2. Spread the asparagus in a single layer on the prepared pan. Drizzle with the oil, season with salt and pepper, and gently toss to coat.

3. In a medium measuring cup, whisk the melted butter, garlic salt, and Italian seasoning.

4. Place the tilapia on the sheet pan. Brush with the butter mixture.

5. Bake for 10 to 12 minutes, or until the fish is cooked through and flakes easily with a fork.

Addition tip: Serve with a side salad or cooked rice for a more filling meal.

FOIL-BAKED SALMON WITH DILL

SERVES 4 | PREP TIME: 10 MINUTES | COOK TIME: 10 MINUTES

5-INGREDIENT | 30-MINUTE | GLUTEN-FREE | NUT-FREE | ONE POT/PAN

This is the recipe that turned my family into salmon lovers. The dill adds an extra special flavor to the fish. Fresh salmon, center cut with the skin still on, tastes best when baked in foil. Serve this with roasted vegetables (see Easy Roasted Vegetables, page 114) for a quick and healthy meal.

Nonstick cooking spray

1 pound skin-on salmon fillets, pin bones removed

1 tablespoon unsalted butter, at room temperature

1 teaspoon Old Bay seasoning

½ teaspoon dried dill weed

½ teaspoon onion powder

1. Preheat the oven to 450°F.

2. Cut two 10-inch-long sheets of foil. Place the first widthwise on a sheet pan. Layer the second sheet over the first lengthwise. Mist with cooking spray.

3. Place the salmon on top of the prepared foil, skin-side down.

4. In a small bowl, combine the butter, Old Bay, dill, and onion powder. Spread the butter mixture over the salmon. Fold the foil over the salmon and seal into a packet.

5. Bake for about 10 minutes, checking the salmon at the 8-minute mark and continuing to cook, as needed. Salmon cooks quickly. The salmon is done when it turns from red to a beautiful pink color and flakes easily with a fork.

QUICK GARLIC BUTTER SHRIMP

SERVES 4 | PREP TIME: 15 MINUTES | COOK TIME: 4 MINUTES

5-INGREDIENT | 30-MINUTE | GLUTEN-FREE | NUT-FREE | ONE POT/PAN

Butter and garlic are the stars of this simple shrimp recipe. With the right combination, you can achieve bold flavors in little time with few ingredients.

8 tablespoons (1 stick) salted butter

4 garlic cloves, minced

¼ teaspoon red pepper flakes

1 pound large (about 30) shrimp, peeled and deveined

Juice of 1 lemon (optional)

1. In a 12-inch skillet, melt the butter over medium heat. Add the garlic and cook for 1 minute, until fragrant.
2. Stir in the red pepper flakes and shrimp, spreading the shrimp into a single layer. Cook for 1 to 2 minutes, or until the shrimp are pink and opaque on the bottom. Flip and cook for 1 to 2 minutes more, until opaque throughout.
3. Squeeze the lemon over the shrimp (if using) and serve.

Addition tip: This shrimp is even more delicious served over pasta or rice, or with a combination of your favorite vegetables. I often sprinkle the shrimp with parsley and add a side of roasted asparagus.

BAKED LEMON COD FILLETS

SERVES 4 | PREP TIME: 10 MINUTES | COOK TIME: 20 MINUTES

30-MINUTE | NUT-FREE

Cod is a great fish to make when you are in a rush and looking for a no-fuss meal. It is an inexpensive, mild, white fish that pairs with almost any flavor. This version features fillets topped with a crumb coating that bakes to a crunchy finish.

4 tablespoons (½ stick) unsalted butter, divided

2 garlic cloves, minced

1 pound cod fillets

Kosher salt

Freshly ground black pepper

1 cup Homemade Bread Crumbs (page 158) or store-bought bread crumbs

1 tablespoon freshly squeezed lemon juice

1 tablespoon chopped fresh parsley

1. Preheat the oven to 400°F.

2. Place 2 tablespoons of butter and the garlic in a 9-by-13-inch baking dish and place the dish in the oven for 1 to 2 minutes, or until the butter melts. Remove the baking dish from the oven and carefully place the fish directly into the butter, turning once to coat. Season with salt and pepper.

3. In a microwave-safe medium measuring cup, melt the remaining 2 tablespoons of butter in the microwave. Stir in the bread crumbs. Divide the buttery crumbs over the top of the fillets. Drizzle with the lemon juice.

4. Bake for 20 minutes, or until the fish is opaque and flakes easily with a fork.

5. Sprinkle with the parsley and serve.

SALSA CHICKEN

SERVES 4 | PREP TIME: 10 MINUTES | COOK TIME: 4 HOURS

5-INGREDIENT | GLUTEN-FREE | NUT-FREE | SLOW COOKER

This flavorful salsa chicken opens the door to so many serving options: Pair it with Mexican-style rice, turn it into a filling for tacos or burritos, or place it on top of a salad! The secret to juicy chicken is to keep the cooking temperature low and cook for about 4 hours.

4 boneless, skinless chicken breasts, fat trimmed

2 tablespoons Taco Seasoning (page 156) or store-bought seasoning

1¼ cups salsa

1 cup shredded pepper Jack cheese

Cooked rice or tortillas, for serving

1. Arrange the chicken in a single layer in a 4-quart slow cooker.
2. Sprinkle 1 tablespoon of taco seasoning over the chicken. Flip each piece and sprinkle with the remaining seasoning. Pour the salsa over the chicken.
3. Cover and cook on Low heat for 3 hours 30 minutes.
4. Sprinkle the cheese over the chicken. Re-cover and cook for about 30 minutes more. Serve over rice or in tortillas, as desired.

Addition tip: Add 1 (15.25-ounce) can corn, drained and rinsed, and 1 (15-ounce) can black beans, drained and rinsed, with the salsa for added flavor.

Ingredient tip: The salsa in this recipe provides big flavor, so use a quality brand. I love Green Mountain Gringo salsas.

SLOW COOKER BARBECUE CHICKEN

SERVES 4 | PREP TIME: 20 MINUTES | COOK TIME: 4 HOURS

DAIRY-FREE | GLUTEN-FREE | NUT-FREE | SLOW COOKER

Serve these chicken breasts with my Southern Corn Bread (page 116) or shred them and make sandwiches. The secret ingredient here? Italian dressing! Use my homemade recipe or a high-quality store brand—stay away from the cheaper varieties.

1½ pounds boneless, skinless chicken breasts, fat trimmed

½ cup chicken broth

½ cup diced onion

3 garlic cloves, minced

2 cups Southern Barbecue Sauce (page 149) or store-bought sauce

½ cup Italian Salad Dressing (page 148) or store-bought dressing

¼ cup packed light brown sugar

2 tablespoons Worcestershire sauce

1. In a 4-quart slow cooker, combine the chicken and chicken broth.
2. Cover and cook on Low heat for 3 hours.
3. Remove the chicken from the slow cooker, shred it if desired, and drain off the juices. Return the chicken (whole or shredded) to the slow cooker. Place the onion on top.
4. In a large measuring cup, stir together the garlic, barbecue sauce, Italian dressing, brown sugar, and Worcestershire sauce. Pour the sauce over the chicken. Re-cover and cook on Low heat for 1 hour more.

Addition tip: This chicken is also great in quesadillas or as a topping on baked potatoes, pizza, or a salad.

Cooking tip: If you use a slow cooker that's larger than 4 quarts, you may need to shorten the cook time or stir occasionally while cooking.

CREAMY TUNA PASTA SALAD

SERVES 4 TO 6 | PREP TIME: 10 MINUTES, PLUS 1 HOUR TO CHILL | COOK TIME: 10 MINUTES

MAKE AHEAD | NUT-FREE

Canned tuna is an often overlooked easy dinner idea. During summer, when it is too hot to turn on the oven, I reach for this pasta salad recipe. It is simple, filling, and perfect for meal prep because it lasts for days! In fact, the longer it sits, the better it tastes.

1 pound rotini pasta

1½ cups mayonnaise

½ cup whole milk

3 tablespoons dill pickle juice

1 teaspoon dried dill weed

½ teaspoon celery salt

¼ teaspoon freshly ground black pepper

2 (5-ounce) cans tuna, drained

½ cup chopped red onion

½ cup chopped celery

1 cup peas

3 hard-boiled eggs, peeled and chopped

1. Cook the pasta according to the package directions until al dente. Drain and set aside.
2. In a large bowl, whisk together the mayonnaise, milk, pickle juice, dill, celery salt, and pepper to combine.
3. Stir in the tuna, red onion, celery, peas, eggs, and pasta. Refrigerate for 1 hour before serving and keep refrigerated for up to 5 days.

Substitution tip: Canned chicken can replace the tuna in this recipe.

GRILLED CHICKEN KEBABS WITH SUMMER VEGETABLES

SERVES 4 | PREP TIME: 20 MINUTES, PLUS 1 HOUR TO MARINATE | COOK TIME: 14 MINUTES

DAIRY-FREE | GLUTEN-FREE | NUT-FREE | ONE POT/PAN

Grilling season is my family's favorite time of year. Kebabs are a simple dinner idea that can be easily customized for your family. We like to use the vegetables listed here, but you can substitute whatever you like or have on hand. Try steak in place of chicken or add mushrooms or corn on the cob to your skewers.

3 boneless, skinless chicken breasts, cut into 1-inch chunks

1 zucchini, cut into 1-inch chunks

1 yellow squash, cut into 1-inch chunks

1 red or green bell pepper, seeded and cut into 1-inch chunks

½ red onion, cut into 1-inch chunks

½ cup sun-dried tomato salad dressing

1. In a gallon-size zip-top bag, combine all the ingredients. Seal the bag and gently shake to coat. Refrigerate at least 1 hour, or up to 8 hours.

2. About 30 minutes before cooking, soak 8 wooden skewers in cold water.

3. Preheat the grill, or a grill pan, to medium-high heat.

4. While the grill preheats, thread the ingredients onto the skewers, alternating the chicken and vegetables.

5. Place the skewers on the grill and cook for 7 minutes per side, or until the chicken reaches an internal temperature of 165°F.

Cooking tip: You can also make these in the oven. Preheat the broiler. Line a sheet pan with aluminum foil and lightly mist with cooking spray. Arrange the threaded kebabs on the pan and broil for 5 minutes per side, or until the chicken is cooked through.

SLOW COOKER ITALIAN CHICKEN AND POTATOES

SERVES 4 | PREP TIME: 10 MINUTES | COOK TIME: 4 HOURS

5-INGREDIENT | GLUTEN-FREE | NUT-FREE | SLOW COOKER

You can never go wrong with chicken and potatoes. Toss a vegetable right into the slow cooker and you have dinner ready in just 4 hours. Add this one to your must-make list.

Nonstick cooking spray

8 tablespoons (1 stick) melted salted butter, divided

2 tablespoons Italian Dressing Seasoning (page 157) or 1 (0.7-ounce) packet Italian dressing mix, divided

1 pound boneless, skinless chicken breasts, fat trimmed

2 cups green beans, trimmed

3 cups quartered red potatoes

1. Mist a 4-quart slow cooker with cooking spray.
2. Spread 2 tablespoons of melted butter onto the chicken and sprinkle with half the seasoning. Place the chicken in the prepared cooker.
3. Place the green beans and potatoes on top of the chicken. Drizzle with the remaining 6 tablespoons of butter and remaining seasoning.
4. Cover and cook on Low heat for 4 hours.

Cooking tip: If you use a slow cooker that's larger than 4 quarts, you may need to shorten the cook time or stir occasionally while cooking.

Variation tip: Substitute broccoli, carrots, or Brussels sprouts for the green beans.

TUNA NOODLE CASSEROLE

SERVES 4 TO 6 | PREP TIME: 10 MINUTES | COOK TIME: 35 MINUTES
NUT-FREE

This dinner recipe is just the thing for cleaning out the pantry. Tuna, cream of mushroom soup, and noodles combine to create the ultimate comfort casserole—and crispy potato chips give it the perfect finish. Since this uses canned tuna, prep time is minimal.

10 ounces egg noodles

Nonstick cooking spray

2 (10.5-ounce) cans cream of mushroom soup

2 (5-ounce) cans tuna, drained

2 cups shredded sharp Cheddar cheese

1 cup frozen peas

½ cup whole milk

¼ cup sour cream

½ red onion, chopped

1 cup potato chips, slightly crushed

1. Cook the noodles according to the package directions until al dente. Drain and set aside.

2. Preheat the oven to 350°F. Mist a 2-quart baking dish with cooking spray.

3. In the prepared baking dish, stir together the noodles, soup, tuna, 1 cup of Cheddar cheese, the peas, milk, sour cream, and red onion. Sprinkle with the remaining cheese and the potato chips.

4. Bake for 20 minutes, or until heated through and the cheese is melted.

Variation tip: Use canned chicken instead of tuna or use butter crackers instead of potato chips. You can also add more vegetables, like corn or canned green beans, if you like.

BEEF AND PORK MAINS

< Apple and Pork Chop Skillet Dinner, p. 111

CHEESY LASAGNA STUFFED SHELLS

SERVES 6 | PREP TIME: 25 MINUTES | COOK TIME: 30 MINUTES

MAKE AHEAD | NUT-FREE

This is a tried-and-true family favorite recipe made with all the ingredients you would see in a traditional lasagna but prepped in half the time. Serve it with a side salad with Homemade Ranch Dressing (page 146) and Easy Baked Garlic Bread (page 118).

20 jumbo pasta shells

2 cups marinara sauce, divided

1 pound Italian sausage or ground beef

¾ cup ricotta

1 cup shredded mozzarella cheese, divided

¼ cup shredded Parmesan cheese

1 large egg

¼ cup frozen spinach, thawed and drained

1. Cook the pasta shells according to the package directions until al dente. Drain and set aside.
2. Preheat the oven to 350°F.
3. Spread ½ cup of marinara sauce in the bottom of a 13-by-9-inch baking dish.
4. In a 10-inch skillet, cook the sausage over medium heat for 5 to 8 minutes, until crumbled and browned. Stir in 1 cup of marinara sauce and set aside.
5. In a small bowl, stir together the ricotta, ½ cup of mozzarella cheese, the Parmesan cheese, egg, and spinach. Stir the cheese mixture into the cooked sausage.
6. Spoon a hearty amount of filling into each and place them in the prepared baking dish.
7. Cover the shells with the remaining ½ cup of marinara and sprinkle with the remaining ½ cup of mozzarella. Cover the baking dish with aluminum foil.
8. Bake for 20 minutes. Remove the foil and bake for 10 minutes more, or until the cheese is melted and bubbling.

Make ahead tip: To freeze, follow the instructions above through step 7. Cover the dish securely with heavy-duty foil or transfer the shells to a freezer-safe container. Take the stuffed shells out of the freezer the day before you plan to cook them and allow them to thaw in the refrigerator. Bake, covered with foil, at 350°F for 45 minutes. Remove the foil and bake for 20 minutes more, or until the cheese is melted and bubbling.

CLASSIC SLOPPY JOES

SERVES 6 | PREP TIME: 15 MINUTES | COOK TIME: 2 TO 8 HOURS

DAIRY-FREE | NUT-FREE | SLOW COOKER

I grew up with sloppy Joes as a dinner staple. Over the years, I have adapted the sloppy Joes of my memory to create a version my family loves. Full of bold tomato flavor and ready for the slow cooker in just 15 minutes, it's my go-to for those weekdays when I'm too busy to spend time in the kitchen.

1 pound ground beef

¾ cup ketchup

½ cup water

¼ cup chopped onion

¼ cup chopped green
bell pepper

1 teaspoon yellow mustard

1 teaspoon Worcestershire
sauce

½ teaspoon garlic powder

Kosher salt

Freshly ground black pepper

6 hamburger buns

1. In a 10-inch skillet, cook the ground beef over medium heat for 5 to 8 minutes, or until crumbled and browned. Transfer the meat to a 4-quart slow cooker.

2. Stir in the ketchup, water, onion, bell pepper, mustard, Worcestershire sauce, and garlic powder. Season with salt and pepper.

3. Cover and cook on High heat for 2 to 4 hours, or on Low heat for 6 to 8 hours. Serve on hamburger buns.

Cooking tip: To make this on the stovetop, cook the ground beef as directed and stir in the remaining ingredients (except the buns). Simmer for 30 minutes and serve on the buns.

MAKE AHEAD BEEF TACOS

SERVES 4 | PREP TIME: 10 MINUTES | COOK TIME: 20 MINUTES

30-MINUTE | MAKE AHEAD | NUT-FREE | ONE POT/PAN

Homemade tacos are special enough to be my birthday dinner request every year, but this recipe is so easy it fits the bill any night you don't want to spend a ton of time in the kitchen. You can even make these in advance as they are very freezer-friendly!

1 pound ground beef

½ cup water

1 tablespoon Taco Seasoning (page 156) or store-bought seasoning

8 (6-inch) flour tortillas

Shredded lettuce, for serving (optional)

Diced tomato, for serving (optional)

Shredded cheese of choice, for serving (optional)

1. In a 10-inch skillet, cook the ground beef over medium heat for 8 to 10 minutes, until crumbled and browned.
2. Stir in the water and taco seasoning. Bring to a simmer and cook for 5 minutes, or until the liquid is reduced.
3. Serve on tortillas with your favorite taco toppings.

Ingredient tip: I prefer to use 80/20 ground beef, but any ratio of lean to fat will work for this recipe.

Make ahead tip: To make ahead, cook the beef mixture through step 2, let cool, then place it in an airtight container or freezer-safe zip-top bag. Freeze for up to 2 months. When ready to eat, remove from the freezer and place in a skillet over medium heat for 5 to 8 minutes, or until heated through. Serve as desired.

Variation tip: My mom makes these tacos with corn tortillas that are lightly fried in oil, and it is delicious.

BEEF AND CHEESE SHEET PAN NACHOS

SERVES 4 | PREP TIME: 10 MINUTES | COOK TIME: 30 MINUTES
NUT-FREE | ONE POT/PAN

I am not ashamed to admit that this recipe makes the regular rounds on our dinner menu rotation. It is a super-simple meal that is easy to customize, which means everyone in the family is happy. The meat-and-bean filling is also delicious when served in burritos or tacos!

Nonstick cooking spray

1 pound ground beef

1 cup diced onion

3 garlic cloves, minced

¼ cup water

1 tablespoon Taco Seasoning (page 156) or store-bought seasoning

1 (16-ounce) can refried beans

9 ounces tortilla chips (about ¾ of a 12-ounce bag)

3 cups shredded sharp Cheddar cheese

Minced jalapeño pepper, for serving (optional)

Diced tomato, for serving (optional)

Sliced black olives, for serving (optional)

Sliced scallions, for serving (optional)

Chopped avocado, for serving (optional)

1. Preheat the oven to 400°F. Line a sheet pan with aluminum foil and mist it with cooking spray. Set aside.

2. In a 10-inch skillet, cook the beef and onion over medium heat for 8 to 10 minutes, or until the onion is soft and the ground beef is crumbled and browned. Stir in the garlic and cook for 1 minute more.

3. Stir in the water and taco seasoning. Simmer for 5 minutes, or until the liquid has reduced. Stir in the refried beans. Remove the skillet from the heat.

4. Spread an even layer of tortilla chips on the prepared sheet pan. Spoon half the meat mixture over the chips. Sprinkle with half the Cheddar cheese. Repeat with another layer of chips, meat, and cheese.

5. Bake for 6 to 10 minutes, or until the cheese has melted. Serve with any toppings you desire.

Cooking tip: Make this a family event. Divide the mixture among smaller sheet pans and let everyone top their own nachos. Little ones will love sprinkling cheese and tomato over their own chips!

TOT CASSEROLE

SERVES 4 TO 6 | PREP TIME: 10 MINUTES | COOK TIME: 20 MINUTES

5-INGREDIENT | NUT-FREE

Twelve years ago, when my husband and I were dating, he invited me to dinner with his parents and I tried tater tot casserole for the first time. In this simple recipe, ground beef is cooked and stirred with a creamed soup and shredded cheese, then spread into a pan and topped with frozen tater tots. Any frozen tot will work, but we especially love Ore-Ida Crispy Crowns. They are thinner and get crispier during the baking process.

1 pound ground beef

1 (10.5-ounce) can cream of mushroom soup or cream of chicken soup

1 cup shredded cheese of choice

2 to 3 cups frozen potato tots

¼ cup diced scallions (optional)

Ketchup, for serving (optional)

1. Preheat the oven to 450°F.

2. In a 10-inch skillet, cook the ground beef over medium heat for about 10 minutes, until crumbled and browned. Stir in the soup and shredded cheese. Pour the beef mixture into a 13-by-9-inch baking dish.

3. Cover the top of the beef mixture evenly with the tots.

4. Bake for 20 minutes, or until the tots are crispy. If desired, sprinkle with scallions and serve with ketchup.

CLASSIC BEEF CHILI

SERVES 4 TO 6 | PREP TIME: 15 MINUTES | COOK TIME: 1 HOUR 15 MINUTES

GLUTEN-FREE | MAKE AHEAD | NUT-FREE | ONE POT/PAN

Chili is the ultimate comfort food, and it always makes a delicious dinner. This recipe is hearty and full of flavor. Try serving it with my Southern Corn Bread (page 116).

1 pound ground beef

1 onion, chopped

½ green bell pepper, seeded and chopped

2 garlic cloves, minced

1 (15-ounce) can pinto beans, drained and rinsed

1 (15-ounce) can kidney beans, drained and rinsed

2 (14.5-ounce) cans diced tomatoes, undrained

2 (4-ounce) cans diced green chilies

1 (8-ounce) can tomato sauce

1½ tablespoons chili powder

1½ teaspoons ground cumin

1 teaspoon kosher salt

1 teaspoon dried oregano

Shredded cheese of choice, for topping (optional)

Sour cream, for topping (optional)

Corn or tortilla chips, for topping (optional)

Sliced scallions, for topping (optional)

1. Heat a large Dutch oven or large pot over medium heat. Add the ground beef, onion, and green bell pepper and cook for about 10 minutes, until the ground beef is crumbled and browned and the onion and pepper are soft. Add the garlic and cook for 1 minute more. Drain any grease. Return the pot to the heat.

2. Stir in the pinto beans, kidney beans, tomatoes and their juices, green chilies, tomato sauce, chili powder, cumin, salt, and oregano. Bring the chili to a simmer and cook over low heat, uncovered, for 1 hour. Serve with toppings (if using).

3. To store leftovers, let cool, then refrigerate in an airtight container for 2 to 3 days.

Cooking tip: To make this chili in a slow cooker, follow step 1, but transfer the cooked, drained beef mixture to a 4-quart slow cooler. Add the remaining ingredients, minus the toppings. Cover and cook on Low heat for 6 hours. Top as desired when serving.

Make ahead tip: To make ahead, follow step 1. Let cool slightly, then transfer the beef mixture to a large freezer-safe zip-top bag and add the remaining ingredients, except the cheese and toppings. Label and freeze for 4 to 6 months. To reheat, put the frozen chili in a large Dutch oven over medium heat. Bring to a simmer and cook over low heat for 1 hour.

BEEF MEATBALLS FOUR WAYS

SERVES 4 | PREP TIME: 20 MINUTES | COOK TIME: 40 MINUTES

MAKE AHEAD | NUT-FREE

Ditch store-bought meatballs and make a large batch of these to elevate your dinner game. I've included our four favorite ways to use them.

Nonstick cooking spray

1 pound ground beef

¼ cup Homemade Bread Crumbs (page 158) or store-bought bread crumbs

2 large eggs

2 tablespoons dried minced onion

2 tablespoons shredded Parmesan cheese

2 garlic cloves, minced

2 teaspoons Italian Seasoning (page 156) or store-bought seasoning

1 teaspoon kosher salt

½ teaspoon freshly ground black pepper

1 (24-ounce) jar marinara sauce

1. Preheat the broiler. Line a large sheet pan with aluminum foil and lightly mist it with cooking spray. Set aside.

2. In a medium bowl, gently mix the ground beef, bread crumbs, eggs, dried onion, Parmesan cheese, garlic, Italian seasoning, salt, and pepper with your hands until combined. Scoop 2 to 3 tablespoons of the meat mixture and roll it into a ball. Place the meatball on the prepared sheet pan. Continue until all the meatballs are rolled and on the tray.

3. Broil for 10 minutes, or until the meatballs are golden brown on top. Transfer the meatballs to a large pot over medium-low heat. Add the marinara sauce and simmer 30 minutes.

VARIATIONS

Spaghetti and Meatballs: Swap half the ground beef for Italian sausage. Follow the recipe as directed. Serve with spaghetti, freshly shredded Parmesan cheese, and basil.

Meatball Sub Sandwich: Substitute Italian-style bread crumbs (see Variation tip, page 158) for the Homemade Bread Crumbs. Follow the recipe as directed. Preheat the broiler. Split a sub roll, spread it with Garlic Butter (page 150), and broil for 3 minutes. Spoon the meatballs and sauce onto the roll and top with a slice of mozzarella cheese. Broil until the cheese is melted.

Meatball Pizza: Quarter the meatballs and use as a topping on Personal Margherita Pizzas (page 56).

SLOW COOKER FRENCH DIP

SERVES 4 TO 6 | PREP TIME: 10 MINUTES | COOK TIME: 8 HOURS

NUT-FREE | SLOW COOKER

These French dip sandwiches are made with the most incredibly tender fall-apart meat layered on a lightly toasted bun and dipped into homemade *jus*. Because there are only a few ingredients, flavor and quality are key. Slow cooking a beef roast for 8 hours gives you a delectable balance of flavors. The combination of beef broth and beer is robust.

½ teaspoon garlic salt

½ teaspoon onion salt

½ teaspoon kosher salt

¼ teaspoon freshly ground black pepper

1 (3-pound) beef roast, such as chuck roast

1 (12-ounce) can good-quality dark beer, such as Guinness

1 (10.5-ounce) can beef broth

1 (10.5-ounce) beef consommé

1 tablespoon Worcestershire sauce

1 teaspoon minced garlic

4 to 6 French sandwich rolls

2 tablespoons unsalted butter, at room temperature

1. In a small bowl, combine the garlic salt, onion salt, kosher salt, and pepper. Sprinkle the spice mix over the roast and place the roast in a 4-quart slow cooker. Add the beer, beef broth, consommé, Worcestershire sauce, and garlic.

2. Cover and cook on Low heat for 8 hours.

3. Strain the liquid into a container and set aside.

4. Preheat the broiler.

5. Using two forks, shred the beef and cover with aluminum foil to keep warm.

6. Split the sandwich rolls and spread the insides with butter. Broil for 2 to 3 minutes, until lightly toasted, watching closely to prevent burning.

7. Fill the toasted buns with the shredded meat and serve with a side of the reserved broth for dipping.

Ingredient tip: I purchase whatever roast is on sale for this recipe.

BALSAMIC PORK ROAST

**SERVES 4 TO 6 | PREP TIME: 20 MINUTES, PLUS AT LEAST 2 HOURS TO MARINATE |
COOK TIME: 1 HOUR**

DAIRY-FREE | GLUTEN-FREE | NUT-FREE | ONE POT/PAN

In this one-pan dinner, pork loin is marinated in a sweet and slightly tangy sauce and baked with carrots, potatoes, and onions. The vinegar helps tenderize the meat and the garlic, honey, and rosemary give it a mouthwatering finish.

½ cup extra-virgin olive oil

¼ cup balsamic vinegar

¼ cup white wine

⅓ cup honey

2 garlic cloves, minced

1 (1½ - to 2-pound) pork loin

Nonstick cooking spray

1 cup whole baby carrots

8 ounces baby potatoes, quartered

1 onion, sliced

Kosher salt

Freshly ground black pepper

Fresh rosemary leaves, for seasoning

1. In a medium bowl, whisk the oil, vinegar, white wine, honey, and garlic to combine. Reserve ¼ cup of marinade, cover, and set aside. Pour the remaining marinade into a large zip-top bag (or container with a secure lid) and add the pork. Seal the bag and refrigerate for at least 2 hours, or for as long as overnight, to marinate.

2. Preheat the oven to 350°F. Mist a 9-by-13-inch baking dish with cooking spray.

3. Place the carrots, potatoes, and onion in the prepared baking dish and pour in the reserved ¼ cup of marinade. Toss the vegetables to coat. Remove the pork from the marinade and place it in the middle of the vegetables and generously season with salt, pepper, and rosemary. Discard the used marinade.

4. Bake for 1 hour, or until the roast reaches an internal temperature of 145°F. Let rest for 10 minutes before slicing and serving.

Cooking tip: This recipe really is best with wine, but you can substitute vegetable broth, if necessary.

CREAMY CHEESEBURGER MACARONI

SERVES 4 | PREP TIME: 15 MINUTES | COOK TIME: 35 MINUTES

NUT-FREE | ONE POT/PAN

Boxed beef and cheese pasta was a meal staple in our home when I was growing up. It was a cheap, easy dinner my mom could have on the table quickly. This is my homemade version of that convenient meal, which my family has quickly grown to love. My healthier version is full of bold cheesy flavor.

8 ounces (about 2 cups) dried elbow macaroni

1 pound ground beef

1 cup diced onion

2 garlic cloves, minced

2 tablespoons all-purpose flour

½ teaspoon kosher salt

¼ teaspoon freshly ground black pepper

2 cups beef broth

2 cups marinara sauce

2 ounces cream cheese

1½ cups shredded sharp Cheddar cheese

¾ cup whole milk

1. Cook the pasta according to the package directions until al dente. Drain the pasta and set aside. Put the pot back on the stovetop.

2. In the same pot, cook the ground beef and onion over medium heat for 5 to 8 minutes, or until the beef is crumbled and browned. Add the garlic and cook for 1 minute more.

3. Add the flour, salt, and pepper and stir until fully incorporated, then stir in the beef broth and marinara. Simmer for 5 to 6 minutes, or until slightly thickened.

4. Add the cream cheese and cook, stirring, just until melted. Stir in the Cheddar cheese and milk. Cook for about 2 minutes, until heated through.

5. Stir in the pasta and cook for about 2 minutes more. Serve warm.

EASY BARBECUE PULLED PORK

SERVES 4 | PREP TIME: 5 MINUTES | COOK TIME: 8 HOURS
5-INGREDIENT | DAIRY-FREE | GLUTEN-FREE | NUT-FREE | SLOW COOKER

Soda is the key ingredient in this slow-cooked pulled pork—it works its fizzy magic to tenderize the meat. We go for root beer, Dr Pepper, or standard Coca-Cola, but any dark soda will do. After cooking all day, the juicy meat just falls apart. Serve on buns with pickles or coleslaw for a picnic-style meal.

½ teaspoon garlic powder

½ teaspoon kosher salt

¼ teaspoon freshly ground black pepper

1 (2- to 3-pound) boneless pork shoulder

2 cups soda, such as root beer, Dr Pepper, or Coca-Cola

2 to 3 cups Southern Barbecue Sauce (page 149) or store-bought sauce

1. In a small bowl, combine the garlic powder, salt, and pepper. Rub the spice mix all over the pork shoulder. Place the pork in a 4- to 6-quart slow cooker. Pour the soda around the sides of the roast.

2. Cover and cook on Low heat for 7 hours.

3. Remove the roast from the slow cooker and, using two forks, shred the meat. Drain the juices from the cooker and return the shredded meat to the pot. Pour in the barbecue sauce. Cover and cook for 1 hour more.

4. Serve on buns with your favorite toppings, as desired.

Ingredient tip: Although any dark soda will work in this recipe, I suggest staying away from diet varieties. The added sugar in the soda is part of what helps tenderize and flavor the pork.

PARMESAN-CRUSTED PORK CHOPS

SERVES 4 | PREP TIME: 10 MINUTES | COOK TIME: 20 MINUTES

5-INGREDIENT | 30-MINUTE | NUT-FREE

The secret to a crisp juicy pork chop is to start with a sear over high heat on the stovetop, then finish in the oven. This method gives you a beautifully crispy outside and perfectly moist center. Serve these chops with my Tomato and Bell Pepper Pasta Salad (page 43) or Slow Cooker Baked Potatoes (page 117) for a complete meal.

2 large eggs

1 tablespoon whole milk

½ cup Italian-seasoned bread crumbs (see Homemade Bread Crumbs, page 158) or store-bought seasoned bread crumbs

⅓ cup grated Parmesan cheese

4 thin-cut boneless pork chops

Nonstick cooking spray

1. Preheat the oven to 400°F.
2. In a shallow bowl, whisk the eggs and milk to blend. Set aside. In another shallow bowl, stir together the bread crumbs and Parmesan cheese. Set aside.
3. Heat a 12-inch oven-safe skillet over medium-high heat.
4. While the pan heats, dip each pork chop, one at a time, into the egg mixture followed by the bread crumbs, being sure to press the crumbs into the pork chop.
5. Mist the heated skillet with cooking spray and add the coated pork chops. Cook for 1 minute per side, or until golden brown.
6. Transfer the skillet to the oven and roast for 15 minutes, or until the internal temperature of the pork reaches 145°F.

Cooking tip: Use an instant-read thermometer to get an accurate internal temperature of the pork. These easy-to-use thermometers can be found in most grocery stores for a reasonable price.

HERB SPOON ROAST

SERVES 4 TO 6 | PREP TIME: 15 MINUTES | COOK TIME: 6 TO 8 HOURS

DAIRY-FREE | GLUTEN-FREE | NUT-FREE | SLOW COOKER

A spoon roast is a cut of beef cooked low and slow until you can cut it with a spoon. So tender and juicy and incredibly simple to make. The secret is a flavorful rub and parchment paper! Adjust the cook time to accommodate the size of your roast—about 2 hours on Low for every 1 pound of roast.

2 tablespoons light brown sugar

1 tablespoon garlic powder

2 teaspoons onion powder

2 teaspoons kosher salt

1 teaspoon freshly ground black pepper

1 teaspoon dried oregano

1 teaspoon dried thyme

1 teaspoon dried parsley

2 teaspoons extra-virgin olive oil

1 (3- to 4-pound) sirloin beef roast

1. In a small bowl, stir together the brown sugar, garlic powder, onion powder, salt, pepper, oregano, thyme, and parsley. Set aside.

2. Spread the oil over the roast, then evenly sprinkle the seasoning mix over the roast and gently rub it in.

3. Place two layers of parchment paper, large enough to wrap the roast, on a clean work surface. Place the roast on the paper and tightly wrap it up. Secure the bundle with heat-safe butcher's twine. Place the parchment-wrapped roast in a 4-quart slow cooker.

4. Cover and cook on Low heat for 6 to 8 hours.

5. Remove the roast from the slow cooker and let sit for 10 minutes before removing the parchment. Slice and serve.

Ingredient tip: Sirloin roast is the best; however, a chuck roast can be used in its place.

HAM AND CHEESE SLIDERS

SERVES 4 TO 6 | PREP TIME: 10 MINUTES | COOK TIME: 20 MINUTES
30-MINUTE | NUT-FREE

These sliders are baked on sweet rolls, but have a slight tang due to the Dijon mustard. And the melted butter poured over the top soaks into the rolls, giving the sandwiches a crisp, buttery finish.

Nonstick cooking spray (optional)

12 small Hawaiian sweet slider buns

24 slices thin-cut deli ham

12 slices Swiss cheese

4 tablespoons (½ stick) salted butter, melted

1½ tablespoons Dijon mustard

¾ teaspoon Worcestershire sauce

1½ teaspoons dried minced onion

1. Preheat the oven to 350°F. Mist a square baking pan with cooking spray, or line it with aluminum foil for easy cleanup. Set aside.

2. Split the slider buns. Place the bottom halves in the prepared pan, cut-side up. Place 2 folded slices of ham on top of each roll. Add 1 halved slice of Swiss cheese to each sandwich. Cover with the top halves of the rolls, cut-side down.

3. In a small bowl or measuring cup, whisk the melted butter, mustard, Worcestershire sauce, and dried onion. Pour the mixture over the rolls. Cover the dish with foil.

4. Bake for 10 minutes. Remove the foil and bake for 10 minutes more, or until the cheese is melted and the tops of the rolls are slightly browned. Serve warm.

CLASSIC MEATLOAF

SERVES 6 | PREP TIME: 15 MINUTES | COOK TIME: 1 HOUR 20 MINUTES

MAKE AHEAD | NUT-FREE

Meatloaf is a classic that is surprisingly easy to make and customize. I serve this with Cheesy Party Potatoes (page 115) and roasted vegetables (see Easy Roasted Vegetables, page 114).

Nonstick cooking spray

1½ pounds ground beef

1 large egg

1 cup diced onion

1 cup whole milk

1 tablespoon Worcestershire sauce

1 cup Homemade Bread Crumbs (page 158) or store-bought bread crumbs

½ teaspoon kosher salt

¼ teaspoon freshly ground black pepper

⅔ cup ketchup

¼ cup packed light brown sugar

2 tablespoons yellow mustard

1. Preheat the oven to 350°F. Mist a 9-by-13-inch baking dish with cooking spray. Set aside.

2. In a large bowl, combine the ground beef, egg, onion, milk, Worcestershire, bread crumbs, salt, and pepper. Gently mix the ingredients with your hands until incorporated. Transfer the meat mixture to the prepared pan, forming it into a loaf roughly 9 by 5 inches.

3. In a medium measuring cup, whisk the ketchup, brown sugar, and mustard until smooth. Spread the sauce over the meatloaf.

4. Bake for 1 hour 20 minutes, or until the center of the meatloaf reaches an internal temperature of 160°F.

Make ahead tip: To prep in advance, make the meatloaf through step 3. Cover and refrigerate overnight, or for up to 12 hours. Bake according to the directions in step 4. To freeze, make as directed through step 2. Wrap the unbaked loaf in plastic wrap and transfer to a large freezer-safe zip-top bag and freeze. When ready to cook, remove the meatloaf from the freezer 24 hours in advance and thaw in the refrigerator. Follow the recipe from step 3.

Variation tip: Use this recipe as your base, and after you make it once, go ahead and tailor the flavors to your taste. Try adding 1 cup of diced mushrooms or bell peppers for a veggie version.

JUICY HOMEMADE BURGERS

SERVES 4 | PREP TIME: 10 MINUTES | COOK TIME: 8 MINUTES

5-INGREDIENT | 30-MINUTE | NUT-FREE

This is a five-star recipe, according to my 11-year-old. He lives for burger night and I was ecstatic to create a burger that he likes as much as the one from his favorite burger joint! I usually make my own hamburger seasoning, but in a pinch, I reach for Traeger Beef Rub. Top the burgers with lettuce, tomato, pickles, and onion for a traditional burger combination.

1 pound ground beef

1 tablespoon Hamburger Seasoning (page 157) or store-bought seasoning

1 teaspoon Worcestershire sauce

4 slices cheese of choice (optional)

4 hamburger buns

1. In a large bowl, mix the ground beef, hamburger seasoning, and Worcestershire sauce. Divide the mixture into 4 equal portions and form each portion into a patty slightly larger than the palm of your hand. The burgers will shrink to the perfect size while cooking. Set aside.

2. Preheat a grill to medium-high heat or preheat your oven's broiler.

3. Grill or broil the burgers for 3 to 4 minutes per side. Immediately top with cheese (if using) and serve on buns.

Addition tip: Butter and toast the buns before adding the burgers for a professional finish.

VEGETABLE BEEF STEW

SERVES 6 | PREP TIME: 20 MINUTES | COOK TIME: 8 TO 10 HOURS

DAIRY-FREE | NUT-FREE | SLOW COOKER

This stew is the ultimate dump-and-go recipe. All the ingredients are combined and slow cooked for 10 hours and the result is a bowl of hearty, heart-warming stew. The meat is juicy and tender and the spices add just the right boost of flavor. Serve it with my Seasoned Dinner Rolls (page 126) or over mashed potatoes.

⅓ cup all-purpose flour

1 teaspoon paprika

½ teaspoon seasoned salt

½ teaspoon freshly ground black pepper

2 pounds beef stew meat, cut into 1-inch cubes

3 russet potatoes, peeled and cut into 1-inch cubes

4 carrots, sliced

1 celery stalk, chopped

1 cup sliced mushrooms

1 small onion, chopped

2 garlic cloves, minced

2 bay leaves

1 tablespoon Worcestershire sauce

1½ cups beef broth

1. In a medium measuring cup, whisk the flour, paprika, seasoned salt, and pepper to combine.

2. Place the stew meat into a 4- to 6-quart slow cooker. Sprinkle with the seasoned flour and toss gently to coat.

3. Add the potatoes, carrots, celery, mushrooms, onion, garlic, bay leaves, and Worcestershire sauce. Pour the beef broth over everything.

4. Cover and cook on Low heat for 8 to 10 hours. Remove the bay leaves before serving.

Cooking tip: This recipe is a great one to use up any leftover vegetables you have on hand, like peas, corn, or bell pepper! Just toss them in with the other vegetables.

Ingredient tip: I like Lawry's Seasoned Salt, which you can easily find in grocery stores.

SHEET PAN SAUSAGE AND VEGGIES

SERVES 4 | PREP TIME: 5 MINUTES | COOK TIME: 30 MINUTES

5-INGREDIENT | DAIRY-FREE | GLUTEN-FREE | NUT-FREE | ONE POT/PAN

Sheet pan dinners are a delight. Whoever came up with the idea to toss everything together on one pan is a genius. With only five ingredients—not counting salt, pepper, and oil—this recipe combines sausage with vegetables and basic seasonings. Roast everything in the oven for a bit and your dinner is served!

Nonstick cooking spray

1 (12-ounce) package chicken sausage or turkey sausage, casings removed, cut into ½-inch pieces

8 ounces green beans, trimmed

2 bell peppers, any color, seeded and quartered

2 cups baby red potatoes, halved

2 to 3 tablespoons extra-virgin olive oil

1½ teaspoons Italian Seasoning (page 156) or store-bought seasoning

¼ teaspoon kosher salt

¼ teaspoon freshly ground black pepper

1. Preheat the oven to 400°F. Line a large sheet pan with aluminum foil and mist it with cooking spray.

2. On the prepared pan, combine the sausage, green beans, bell peppers, and potatoes. Drizzle with the oil and toss to coat. Spread the ingredients into a single layer and sprinkle with the Italian seasoning, salt, and pepper.

3. Bake for 15 minutes, stir, and bake for 15 minutes more, or until the vegetables are soft and the sausage is browned.

Variation tip: Try flavored sausages! My family loves pineapple-bacon chicken sausage.

SLOW COOKER SHEPHERD'S PIE

SERVES 4 | PREP TIME: 15 MINUTES | COOK TIME: 4 HOURS 10 MINUTES

NUT-FREE | SLOW COOKER

Shepherd's pie, also known as cottage pie, is a basic yet incredibly satisfying dinner. It combines cooked ground red meat (I use beef here), vegetables, and mashed potatoes into a single casserole. If you are short on time, prepare this in a baking dish and bake it in the oven at 400°F for 30 minutes.

1½ pounds ground beef

½ cup beef broth

1 tablespoon tomato paste

1 teaspoon Worcestershire sauce

½ teaspoon kosher salt

¼ teaspoon freshly ground black pepper

1½ cups chopped onion

½ cup diced carrot

½ cup sweet corn

½ cup peas

3 cups homemade mashed potatoes or 1 (24-ounce) package store-bought mashed potatoes

1 cup shredded Cheddar cheese

1. In a 12-inch skillet, cook the ground beef over medium heat for about 10 minutes, until crumbled and browned. Drain the grease and transfer the beef to a 4-quart slow cooker.

2. Stir in the beef broth, tomato paste, Worcestershire sauce, salt, and pepper.

3. Stir in the onion, carrot, corn, and peas. Spread the mashed potatoes over the top of the meat mixture.

4. Cover and cook on Low heat for 4 hours.

5. Sprinkle the potatoes with the cheese and cook, covered, for 10 minutes more, or until the cheese is melted.

Make ahead tip: Cook the ground beef ahead of time, let cool, and freeze in an airtight container. Thaw in the refrigerator overnight before using. When you are ready to make shepherd's pie, add the thawed ground beef to the slow cooker, then begin with step 2.

APPLE AND PORK CHOP SKILLET DINNER

SERVES 3 OR 4 | PREP TIME: 10 MINUTES | COOK TIME: 35 MINUTES

NUT-FREE | ONE POT/PAN

Combining sweet with savory makes a very pleasing meal. The slightly tart, slightly sweet Granny Smith apple combined with the salty pork and savory stuffing creates a dish that even the pickiest eater won't be able to resist!

1 tablespoon extra-virgin olive oil

3 or 4 boneless pork chops (1 inch thick)

Kosher salt

Freshly ground black pepper

½ onion, sliced

1 cup water

4 tablespoons (½ stick) unsalted butter

1 (6-ounce) box pork stuffing mix, unprepared

1 Granny Smith apple, unpeeled, cored, and sliced

2 tablespoons light brown sugar

1. Preheat the oven to 350°F.

2. Heat a 12-inch oven-safe skillet over medium heat. Add the oil and heat it until it shimmers.

3. Season the pork chops all over with salt and pepper. Carefully place the pork chops and onion in the skillet. Cook the chops for 2 minutes per side, or until the pork is just browned and the onion is soft. Remove the pork chops and onion and set aside.

4. Into the same skillet, stir the water and butter and bring to a boil. Add the stuffing mix and the cooked onion. Stir to combine. Top with the pork chops.

5. In a small bowl, toss together the apple and brown sugar. Sprinkle the apples over the pork and stuffing.

6. Bake for 20 to 30 minutes, or until the pork chops are cooked to an internal temperature of 145°F.

SNACKS AND SIDES

< Easy Roasted Vegetables, p. 114

EASY ROASTED VEGETABLES

SERVES 4 | PREP TIME: 10 MINUTES | COOK TIME: 30 MINUTES

5-INGREDIENT | DAIRY-FREE | GLUTEN-FREE | NUT-FREE

This is the easiest way to roast vegetables. These veggies make a quick and healthy side dish to any meal. Following are the basic roasting instructions along with some vegetable combinations my family enjoys.

Nonstick cooking spray

2 tablespoons extra-virgin olive oil

2 tablespoons balsamic vinegar

4 garlic cloves, minced

1 teaspoon Italian Seasoning (page 156) or store-bought seasoning

½ teaspoon kosher salt

¼ teaspoon freshly ground black pepper

6 cups mixed vegetables, sliced or cubed into 1-inch pieces

1. Preheat the oven to 425°F. Mist a sheet pan with cooking spray.
2. In a small measuring cup, whisk the oil, vinegar, garlic, Italian seasoning, salt, and pepper to combine.
3. Place the vegetables in a large bowl and drizzle the dressing over the vegetables. Toss to coat. If using root vegetables, like potatoes, add them to the prepared sheet pan. Set the other, nonroot, vegetables aside.
4. Bake the root vegetables for 15 minutes.
5. Add all the other vegetables to the sheet pan, stir, and bake for 12 to 15 minutes more, or until hot and tender.

ROASTED VEGETABLES COMBINATION 1:

2 cups cubed red potatoes

1½ cups green beans

1½ cups broccoli florets

1 cup sliced carrot

ROASTED VEGETABLES COMBINATION 2:

2 cups broccoli florets

1½ cups diced bell pepper, any color

1½ cup sliced mushrooms

1 cup sliced onion

ROASTED VEGETABLES COMBINATION 3:

2 cups broccoli florets

2 cups sliced mushrooms

1 cup cubed zucchini

1 cup sliced onion

CHEESY PARTY POTATOES

SERVES 4 TO 6 | PREP TIME: 15 MINUTES | COOK TIME: 4 HOURS

MAKE AHEAD | NUT-FREE | SLOW COOKER

Often made to share at large gatherings, these cheesy potatoes are a fun side dish for any meal. The best part is that you can make this ahead and let it cook in the slow cooker, making it perfect for parties or potlucks. Be sure to use sharp Cheddar for that bold cheesy taste.

Nonstick cooking spray

1 (28-ounce) bag frozen diced breakfast potatoes, thawed

⅓ cup diced scallions

2 cups shredded sharp Cheddar cheese

2 (10.5-ounce) cans cream of chicken soup

2 cups sour cream

1 teaspoon kosher salt

¼ teaspoon freshly ground black pepper

2 cups crushed corn flakes or potato chips

2 tablespoons unsalted butter, melted

1. Mist a 4-quart slow cooker with cooking spray.

2. In the prepared cooker, stir together the potatoes, scallions, Cheddar cheese, cream of chicken soup, sour cream, salt, and pepper.

3. Cover and cook on High heat for 3 hours, stirring halfway through the cooking time, if possible.

4. In a medium bowl, toss together the corn flakes and melted butter. Sprinkle the buttered flakes over the potatoes. Re-cover and cook for 1 hour more.

Cooking tip: To make this in the oven, use frozen shredded hash browns, thawed, instead of breakfast potatoes. (1) Preheat the oven to 350°F. (2) In a large bowl, stir together the hash browns, scallions, Cheddar cheese, cream of chicken soup, sour cream, salt, and pepper. Transfer to a 9-by-13-inch baking dish. (3) Bake for 45 minutes, or until bubbling. (4) In a medium bowl, toss together the corn flakes and melted butter. Sprinkle the crumbs over the potatoes. Bake for 10 to 15 minutes more, or until the topping is crispy.

SOUTHERN CORN BREAD

SERVES 6 | PREP TIME: 10 MINUTES | COOK TIME: 25 MINUTES

MAKE AHEAD | NUT-FREE

There is nothing better than a slice of warm corn bread smothered with butter and honey. This bread can be made up to 2 days ahead and stored in an airtight container on the countertop. You can also mix the dry ingredients ahead of time and keep them stored in the pantry for a quick grab-and-go corn bread mix!

Nonstick cooking spray

1 cup all-purpose flour

1 cup cornmeal

½ cup sugar

2 teaspoons baking powder

1 teaspoon kosher salt

1 large egg

1 cup whole milk

⅓ cup vegetable oil

Butter, for serving

Honey, for serving

1. Preheat the oven to 400°F. Mist a square baking dish with cooking spray. Set aside.

2. In a medium bowl, whisk the flour, cornmeal, sugar, baking powder, and salt to combine. Set aside.

3. In a medium measuring cup, stir together the egg, milk, and oil. Pour the wet ingredients into the dry ingredients and gently mix by hand until combined. Transfer the batter to the prepared baking dish.

4. Bake for 20 to 25 minutes, or until a toothpick inserted into the center of the bread comes out clean. Let cool slightly before slicing. Serve with butter and honey.

Cooking tip: Corn bread needs to be mixed gently by hand, as overmixing can lead to a dry cake. Mix only until the dry ingredients are just incorporated with the wet ingredients; small lumps in the batter are okay.

Make ahead tip: Bake the corn bread as directed and cool completely. Remove the bread from the pan and tightly wrap it in plastic wrap. Place the wrapped bread in a freezer-safe zip-top bag and freeze for up to 2 months. When you're ready to eat, place the bread the countertop for 20 minutes to thaw slightly. Reheat in a 350°F oven for 5 to 10 minutes, or until warm.

SLOW COOKER BAKED POTATOES

SERVES 6 | PREP TIME: 10 MINUTES | COOK TIME: 4 TO 6 HOURS

5-INGREDIENT | GLUTEN-FREE | NUT-FREE | SLOW COOKER

This recipe makes potatoes with a crispy exterior and a deliciously soft middle. Top with butter or sour cream.

6 large russet potatoes

6 tablespoons (¾ stick) unsalted butter

½ teaspoon kosher salt

1. Wash the potatoes and dry with a paper towel. Prick them with a fork all over to let steam escape while cooking.
2. Rub each potato with 1 tablespoon of butter and sprinkle with salt.
3. Tightly wrap each potato in aluminum foil. Place the wrapped potatoes in a 4-quart slow cooker, stacking them if they do not fit in a single layer.
4. Cover and cook on High heat for 4 hours, or on Low heat for 6 hours.

Variation tip: For a quick wholesome meal, top the potatoes with cooked broccoli and Cheddar Cheese Sauce (page 127), Classic Beef Chili (page 97), or Easy Barbecue Pulled Pork (page 102).

EASY BAKED GARLIC BREAD

SERVES 6 | PREP TIME: 10 MINUTES | COOK TIME: 20 MINUTES

5-INGREDIENT | 30-MINUTE | NUT-FREE

Nothing rounds out a meal like garlic bread! This recipe is simple to make and delivers an unbeatable cheesy garlic flavor. Serve with my Spinach and Cheese Ravioli Bake (page 59) or Italian Sausage Lasagna Soup (page 31).

½ cup Garlic Butter (page 150)

¼ cup grated Parmesan cheese

1 tablespoon chopped fresh parsley

1 loaf French bread, halved horizontally

1. Preheat the oven to 350°F.

2. In a small bowl, stir together the garlic butter, Parmesan cheese, and parsley until well incorporated.

3. Spread the mixture onto both cut sides of the loaf. Put the halves together, cut-sides in, to form a single loaf. Tightly wrap the loaf in aluminum foil.

4. Bake for 15 to 20 minutes, or until the bread is warmed through and the butter is melted.

Variation tip: French bread will give you the classic garlic bread look and taste you know and love, but this spread is great on any style loaf. Try Italian bread, sourdough, or even thick-sliced toast or bagels!

CLASSIC COLESLAW

SERVES 6 | PREP TIME: 15 MINUTES

5-INGREDIENT | 30-MINUTE | DAIRY-FREE | GLUTEN-FREE | NUT-FREE | ONE POT/PAN

Coleslaw is the ideal summer side dish. The creamy but slightly tangy dressing and the crunchy cabbage make it a pleasing companion for all your grilling favorites. Serve it with hot dogs, Easy Barbecue Pulled Pork (page 102), and pork tacos.

½ cup mayonnaise

2 tablespoons sugar

Juice of 1 lemon (about 2 tablespoons)

1 tablespoon distilled white vinegar

¼ teaspoon kosher salt

½ teaspoon freshly ground black pepper

1 (14-ounce) bag coleslaw mix

In a large bowl, whisk the mayonnaise, sugar, lemon juice, vinegar, salt, and pepper until blended. Add the coleslaw mix and toss until coated. Refrigerate until ready to use, or for 3 to 5 days in an airtight container. Serve chilled.

Ingredient tip: Coleslaw mix is found near the bagged lettuce in most local grocery stores. You can also make your own by shredding half of a cabbage and two large carrots.

RESTAURANT-STYLE REFRIED BEANS

SERVES 4 TO 6 | PREP TIME: 10 MINUTES | COOK TIME: 10 MINUTES

5-INGREDIENT | 30-MINUTE | GLUTEN-FREE | NUT-FREE | ONE POT/PAN

I have been making this recipe for years. It is so simple and is regularly requested in my home as a side dish or snack. To make these restaurant-style beans, kick regular refried beans up a notch with sour cream and hot sauce. Top things off with melted cheese and a little chopped scallion and you will not even believe it all started with a can!

1 (16-ounce) can refried beans

¼ cup sour cream

1 tablespoon hot sauce

½ cup shredded
Cheddar cheese

2 tablespoons chopped scallion
(optional)

1. In a medium saucepan, stir together the beans, sour cream, and hot sauce. Cook over medium-low for 5 minutes, or until warm, stirring constantly to avoid burning.

2. Sprinkle the beans with the Cheddar cheese and cover the pan. Cook until the cheese melts, about 1 minute more, then remove from the heat.

3. Sprinkle with the scallion (if using) and serve.

Cooking tip: Make this in the oven. In a medium bowl, stir together the beans, sour cream, and hot sauce. Spread the mixture into a square baking dish, sprinkle with the cheese, and bake at 375°F for 5 to 8 minutes, or until heated through. Sprinkle with the scallion (if using) and serve with Baked Tortilla Chips (opposite page) for dipping.

BAKED TORTILLA CHIPS

SERVES 4 | PREP TIME: 10 MINUTES | COOK TIME: 15 MINUTES

5-INGREDIENT | 30-MINUTE | DAIRY-FREE | GLUTEN-FREE | NUT-FREE | ONE POT/PAN

Making your own tortilla chips is a snap. All you need are tortillas, vegetable oil, and a little salt. Be sure to flip the tortillas halfway through for even baking and you'll have crisp chips that are just right for Restaurant-Style Refried Beans (opposite page), 15-Minute Red Salsa (page 124), Queso con Carne (page 122), or Homemade Guacamole (page 123).

Nonstick cooking spray

1 (12-ounce) package taco-size (4-inch) white corn tortillas

1 tablespoon vegetable oil

1 teaspoon kosher salt

1. Preheat the oven to 350°F. Line a large sheet pan with aluminum foil and mist it with cooking spray. Set aside.
2. Brush each tortilla on both sides with the oil. Stack the coated tortillas on a cutting board. Using a sharp knife or pizza cutter, cut the stack into 8 triangles. Spread the tortillas in a single layer on the prepared baking sheet. Sprinkle with the salt.
3. Bake for 7 minutes. Flip each chip and bake for 7 minutes more, until they are crisp but not browned.

Cooking tip: Watch the baking chips carefully. Determining doneness can be tricky; once they are browned, they are already burnt. After you make this recipe once or twice, you'll know the best bake time for your oven.

Ingredient tip: I like white corn tortillas for this recipe, but flour tortillas will work, too, if you do not need your chips to be gluten-free.

QUESTO CON CARNE

SERVES 10 | PREP TIME: 10 MINUTES | COOK TIME: 4 HOURS

GLUTEN-FREE | MAKE AHEAD | NUT-FREE | SLOW COOKER

This queso is as easy as mixing the ingredients and walking away. The key to bold flavor is a quality salsa. My family loves Trader Joe's Hatch Valley Salsa. Fair warning: This queso is so good, you will not be able to stop eating it.

1 (15-ounce) can chili con carne (chili without beans, like Hormel brand)

1 cup diced onion

1 cup green salsa

12 ounces Velveeta, cubed

2 garlic cloves, minced

1 tablespoon diced pickled jalapeño pepper

Baked Tortilla Chips (page 121), for serving

1. In a 2-quart slow cooker (see the slow cooker tip in the Tools and Equipment section of chapter 1, page 5), stir together the chili, onion, salsa, Velveeta, garlic, and jalapeño.

2. Cover and cook on Low heat for 4 hours. Serve with the tortilla chips.

Cooking tip: This recipe can also be made on the stovetop. In a medium saucepan, stir together all the ingredients. Cook over medium-low heat for 8 to 10 minutes, or until the cheese has melted completely.

Make ahead tip: You can make this dip 3 to 5 days in advance and keep refrigerated in an airtight container. Reheat in the microwave on high power for 30 seconds, stir, and heat for 30 seconds more, or until hot.

HOMEMADE GUACAMOLE

SERVES 4 | PREP TIME: 15 MINUTES

30-MINUTE | DAIRY-FREE | GLUTEN-FREE | NUT-FREE | ONE POT/PAN

I have been obsessed with avocados for as long as I can remember. There are so many great ways you can use them, but my all-time favorite is guacamole. This recipe comes together quickly, but the secret is to not overmash the avocado. Small chunks add the texture that is key to this dip. Serve with Baked Tortilla Chips (page 121) or as a topping on Go-To Grilled Chicken (page 72).

4 ripe avocados, halved and pitted

2 tablespoons freshly squeezed lime juice (from about 1 large lime)

½ teaspoon kosher salt

¼ teaspoon ground cumin

½ cup finely diced red onion

2 garlic cloves, minced

1 jalapeño pepper, seeded and diced

3 tablespoons chopped fresh cilantro

1. Scoop the avocado flesh into a medium bowl and add the lime juice, salt, and cumin. Using a fork, lightly mash the avocado, leaving some chunks for texture.

2. Stir in the red onion, garlic, jalapeño pepper, and cilantro.

Storage tip: Keep an avocado pit in the guacamole to help slow the natural browning that occurs from oxidation. Your guac will stay fresh for 2 days in an airtight container in the refrigerator.

15-MINUTE RED SALSA

SERVES 4 TO 6 | PREP TIME: 15 MINUTES, PLUS 1 HOUR TO CHILL

DAIRY-FREE | GLUTEN-FREE | MAKE AHEAD | NUT-FREE | ONE POT/PAN

Ready for the easiest salsa recipe of all time? Canned tomatoes make this salsa a snap! Bonus: This dip tastes better over time, making it an ideal make ahead recipe!

1 (10-ounce) can diced tomatoes and green chilies, undrained

1 (14.5-ounce) can diced tomatoes, undrained

¼ cup chopped onion

1 garlic clove, peeled

1 jalapeño pepper, seeded and chopped

Small handful fresh cilantro (about ¼ cup), or to taste

Juice of 1 lime

¼ teaspoon kosher salt, plus more as needed

⅛ teaspoon ground cumin, plus more as needed

⅛ teaspoon sugar

1. In a blender or food processor, combine the tomatoes and green chilies and their juices, diced tomatoes and their juices, onion, garlic, jalapeño pepper, cilantro, lime juice, salt, cumin, and sugar. Pulse until combined. I find that 4 or 5 pulses create a great consistency. You want the texture of a thick soup. Taste and add more salt or cumin, as needed.

2. Cover and chill for at least 1 hour before serving. Refrigerate in an airtight container for up to 5 days.

Ingredient tip: I love cilantro, but it has a powerful flavor. If you're not as big a fan as I am, start with half the amount called for in the recipe, taste, and add more as desired.

CREAMY GARLIC HUMMUS

SERVES 4 | PREP TIME: 15 MINUTES

30-MINUTE | DAIRY-FREE | GLUTEN-FREE | MAKE AHEAD | ONE POT/PAN

Hummus is a quick and delicious dip or spread made from chickpeas. Tahini, a ground toasted sesame paste, and fresh garlic provide most of the flavor. If you have never made your own, this is a great beginner's recipe.

¼ cup tahini

2 tablespoons extra-virgin olive oil, plus more for drizzling

1 (15-ounce) can chickpeas, drained and rinsed, liquid reserved

2 tablespoons freshly squeezed lemon juice

1 garlic clove, minced

¼ teaspoon kosher salt, plus more as needed

½ teaspoon paprika (optional)

Toasted pine nuts, for garnish (optional)

1. In a food processor or high-powered blender, combine the tahini and oil. Pulse for 30 seconds to 1 minute, or until smooth.

2. Add the chickpeas, ¼ cup of reserved chickpea liquid, the lemon juice, garlic, and salt. Process for 30 seconds, or until the desired texture is reached, stopping to scrape down the sides of the processor, as needed. If your hummus is too thick, add 1 to 2 teaspoons more oil. Taste and add more salt, if needed.

3. Drizzle with oil before serving. If desired, garnish with paprika and toasted pine nuts. Refrigerate any leftovers in an airtight container for up to 1 week.

Cooking tip: Want to make your own tahini? In a food processor or high-powered blender, combine 1 cup lightly toasted white sesame seeds and ¼ cup extra-virgin olive oil. Pulse for 2 to 3 minutes until smooth. The tahini will stay fresh, refrigerated in an airtight container, for up to 30 days.

Ingredient tip: Tahini will separate as it sits. When you open a new jar, use a small spatula to stir the oil into the paste until smooth.

SEASONED DINNER ROLLS

SERVES 6 | PREP TIME: 10 MINUTES, PLUS 2 HOURS TO RISE | COOK TIME: 20 MINUTES

5-INGREDIENT | NUT-FREE | ONE POT/PAN

This easy seasoned dinner roll is a welcome addition to any meal. Frozen roll dough is brushed with butter and sprinkled with seasoning. Let the dough rise until doubled before baking to a crisp golden brown. Active working time is less than 10 minutes, which means you can focus on other parts of meal prep while the rolls do their thing.

Nonstick cooking spray

6 frozen dough rolls

2 tablespoons salted butter, melted

2 teaspoons Salad Sprinkle (page 156)

1. Mist a small sheet pan, or 9-inch square baking pan, with cooking spray. Arrange the rolls in the prepared pan, spacing them ½ inch apart.

2. Brush each roll with melted butter and top with Salad Sprinkle. Cover the rolls loosely with a clean kitchen towel or plastic wrap and let rise for 2 hours, or until doubled in size.

3. Preheat the oven to 350°F.

4. Bake the rolls for 15 to 20 minutes, or until golden brown.

CHEDDAR CHEESE SAUCE

SERVES 4 | PREP TIME: 10 MINUTES | COOK TIME: 10 MINUTES
5-INGREDIENT | 30-MINUTE | NUT-FREE | ONE POT/PAN

This creamy sauce is silky smooth and packed with cheesy goodness. Try it over roasted vegetables (see Easy Roasted Vegetables, page 114), Slow Cooker Baked Potatoes (page 117), open-faced sandwiches, or even pasta! Be sure to use block cheese that you shred yourself to get that velvety finish.

2 tablespoons unsalted butter

2 tablespoons all-purpose flour

1¼ cups whole milk

1 cup shredded sharp Cheddar cheese

¼ teaspoon salt

¼ teaspoon hot sauce

1. In a medium skillet, heat the butter over medium heat just until melted.
2. Whisk in the flour until a paste forms.
3. While whisking constantly, slowly add the milk, incorporating it into the flour mixture until completely smooth. Bring to a simmer.
4. Remove from the heat and whisk in the Cheddar cheese, salt, and hot sauce. Return to the heat and cook until the cheese melts and the mixture is smooth, whisking constantly to avoid burning.

Variation tip: For a spicy nacho sauce, substitute 1 tablespoon Taco Seasoning (page 156) for the salt and stir in 3 tablespoons diced pickled jalapeño pepper with the cheese.

BAKED SWEET POTATOES WITH HONEY-CINNAMON BUTTER

SERVES 6 | PREP TIME: 15 MINUTES | COOK TIME: 4 TO 6 HOURS

5-INGREDIENT | GLUTEN-FREE | NUT-FREE | SLOW COOKER

Sweet potatoes are delicious no matter how you serve them, but my family's favorite version is smothered in honey-cinnamon butter! This colorful treat is delicious as a side with my Easy Barbecue Pulled Pork (page 102).

6 sweet potatoes

8 tablespoons (1 stick) salted butter, at room temperature

3 tablespoons honey

¼ teaspoon ground cinnamon

1. Wash the sweet potatoes and dry them with a paper towel. Prick the potatoes all over with a fork to let steam escape while cooking. Tightly wrap each potato in a sheet of aluminum foil. Place the wrapped sweet potatoes in a 4-quart slow cooker, stacking them if they do not fit in a single layer.

2. Cover and cook on High heat for 4 hours, or on Low heat for 6 hours, until the potatoes are fork-tender. Remove from the foil.

3. In a medium bowl, using a hand mixer, beat together the butter, honey, and cinnamon until fully incorporated. Spread on the cooked potatoes and enjoy!

Storage tip: Refrigerate the honey-cinnamon butter in an airtight container for up to 1 month. Serve it on pancakes, biscuits, or waffles.

DESSERTS

< Chocolate Sandwich Cookie Truffles, p. 141

PERFECT CHOCOLATE CHIP COOKIES

MAKES 12 TO 15 COOKIES | PREP TIME: 20 MINUTES, PLUS 4 HOURS TO CHILL | COOK TIME: 17 MINUTES

MAKE AHEAD | NUT-FREE

This recipe has taken me years to perfect. Now, I make it every other week and the cookies do not last long in our home. The best part is you can make a batch in advance and keep the dough in the freezer. That means you can have warm, freshly baked cookies in no time. Pro tip: Make sure all the ingredients are at room temperature before starting. This helps everything incorporate easily without overmixing the dough.

1½ cups all-purpose flour

1½ cups cake flour

½ teaspoon baking soda

½ teaspoon kosher salt

12 tablespoons (1½ sticks) unsalted butter, at room temperature

¾ cup packed light brown sugar

½ cup granulated sugar

1 tablespoon pure vanilla extract

2 large eggs

1 cup semisweet or milk chocolate chips

1. In a large measuring cup or bowl, whisk the all-purpose flour, cake flour, baking soda, and salt to combine. Set aside.

2. In the bowl of a stand mixer fitted with the paddle attachment, or in a large bowl using a hand mixer, beat the butter, brown sugar, and granulated sugar on medium-low speed for 2 minutes until slightly fluffy.

3. On low speed, mix in the vanilla, then the eggs, one at a time, just until incorporated.

4. Beat in the dry ingredients just until incorporated. Fold in the chocolate chips. Cover the dough and chill for at least 4 hours, or overnight.

5. Preheat the oven to 325°F. Line 2 baking sheets with parchment paper.

6. Scoop the dough by the ¼ cup onto the prepared baking sheets, spacing the cookies 2 to 3 inches apart. You should get 12 to 15 cookies.

7. Bake for 15 to 17 minutes, or until the edges are slightly curled and browned and the tops no longer look doughy.

8. Cool the cookies completely on the baking sheets—
   except for the one I insist you try fresh from the oven.
   Store leftovers in an airtight container or zip-top bag
   at room temperature for up to 1 week.

Cooking tip: No cake flour? Put 2 tablespoons cornstarch in a
1-cup measuring cup and top it off with all-purpose flour to make
1 cup of cake flour.

Make ahead tip: Roll your dough into ¼-cup balls and place on a
baking sheet. Place the sheet in the freezer for 20 minutes to chill
the dough. Place the chilled cookie dough balls in a heavy-duty
freezer-safe zip-top bag. Freeze until solid. When ready to bake,
pull the cookies out of the freezer and place them on a parchment-
lined baking sheet. Let sit for 20 minutes to thaw, then bake as
directed.

TRIED-AND-TRUE BROWNIES

MAKES 9 TO 12 BROWNIES | PREP TIME: 15 MINUTES | COOK TIME: 35 MINUTES

MAKE AHEAD | NUT-FREE

We are a divided household when it comes to the ideal brownie texture. These fall right in between cakelike and fudgy. For my family, it is the best of both worlds!

Nonstick baking spray

1 cup (2 sticks) unsalted butter, at room temperature

¾ cup granulated sugar

¾ cup packed light brown sugar

1 tablespoon pure vanilla extract

3 large eggs

1 cup all-purpose flour

¾ cup cocoa powder

½ teaspoon baking powder

¼ teaspoon kosher salt

1. Preheat the oven to 350°F. Lightly mist a 9-by-13-inch baking dish with baking spray. Set aside.

2. In a large bowl, whisk the butter, granulated sugar, and brown sugar for about 2 minutes until fluffy and light.

3. Add the vanilla and eggs and stir until combined.

4. In a medium measuring cup, whisk the flour, cocoa powder, baking powder, and salt to combine. Stir the dry ingredients into the wet ingredients and mix until combined. Pour the batter into the prepared pan.

5. Bake for 30 to 35 minutes, or until a toothpick inserted into the center of the brownies comes out clean. Cool, then cut into 9 to 12 bars to serve. Cover and keep at room temperature for 1 to 2 days.

Cooking tip: This recipe tastes best when the ingredients are mixed by hand.

MICROWAVE CHOCOLATE MUG CAKE

SERVES 1 | PREP TIME: 2 MINUTES | COOK TIME: 2 MINUTES

30-MINUTE | ONE POT/PAN

This mug cake takes a total of roughly five minutes and uses ingredients found in most kitchens. The secret to this moist and chocolate-filled treat is the chocolate-hazelnut spread! This recipe yields batter that fits in a 16-ounce mug; if you only have smaller mugs, mix everything in a bowl and evenly divide the batter between two mugs.

¼ cup all-purpose flour

¼ cup sugar

3 tablespoons cocoa powder

3 tablespoons chocolate-hazelnut spread

3 tablespoons whole milk

3 tablespoons vegetable oil

1 large egg

¼ teaspoon baking powder

Pinch kosher salt

1. In a large mug, combine the flour, sugar, cocoa powder, chocolate-hazelnut spread, milk, oil, egg, baking powder, and salt. Using a fork, whisk until fully combined.

2. Microwave on high power for 2 minutes, checking doneness at 90 seconds, until the cake is cooked through and a toothpick inserted into the center comes out clean.

CHOCOLATE-PEANUT BUTTER BARS

**MAKES 9 TO 12 BARS | PREP TIME: 10 MINUTES, PLUS 15 MINUTES TO CHILL |
COOK TIME: 5 MINUTES, PLUS 10 MINUTES TO SET**

5-INGREDIENT | MAKE AHEAD

Sometimes called Lunch Lady Bars, these easy peanut butter bars combine a sweet peanut butter crust with a thin layer of chocolate and taste just like peanut butter cups. With only five ingredients, these are easy enough to make often and share.

Nonstick baking spray (optional)

1 cup (2 sticks) unsalted butter, plus more (optional) for preparing the pan

1¼ cups creamy peanut butter, divided

2 cups graham cracker crumbs

2 cups powdered sugar

1½ cups semisweet or milk chocolate chips

1. Prepare a 9-by-13-inch baking dish by misting it with baking spray, coating with butter, or lining with parchment paper. Set aside.

2. In a microwave-safe medium bowl, combine the butter and 1 cup of peanut butter. Heat on high power for 1 minute, stir, and heat for 30 seconds more, or until fully melted.

3. Stir in the graham cracker crumbs and powdered sugar. Transfer the dough to the prepared baking dish and gently press it down into an even layer. Chill the crust for 15 minutes.

4. In a small microwave-safe bowl, combine the chocolate chips and remaining ¼ cup of peanut butter. Heat on high power in 15- to 30-second intervals, stirring after each, until fully melted. Pour the melted chocolate over the prepared crust. Use a spatula or spoon to spread the chocolate over the bars.

5. Let the chocolate firm up for about 10 minutes. Cut into 9 to 12 bars to serve.

Storage tip: Store leftovers (if there are any!) covered, in the refrigerator or at room temperature for up to 1 week.

Variation tip: Substitute round butter crackers for the graham crackers for a fun variation.

MARSHMALLOW CEREAL TREATS

MAKES 9 TO 12 BARS | PREP TIME: 5 MINUTES | COOK TIME: 10 MINUTES, PLUS 10 MINUTES TO REST

5-INGREDIENT | 30-MINUTE | MAKE AHEAD | NUT-FREE

This classic treat is made with only three ingredients and can be stored in the freezer for up to six weeks. Although these are similar to the store-bought version, the extra butter sends them over the edge. I use Rice Krispies in this recipe, but feel free to get creative with your favorite cereal variety.

Nonstick baking spray (optional)

6 tablespoons (¾ stick) salted butter, plus more (optional) for preparing the pan

1 (10-ounce) bag mini marshmallows

6 cups puffed rice cereal (I like Rice Krispies)

1. Prepare a 9-by-13-inch baking dish by misting it with baking spray or coating with butter.

2. In a large pot, melt the butter over medium-low heat. Using a silicone spatula, stir in the marshmallows and cook, stirring, until melted.

3. Working quickly, add the cereal to the pot and stir to combine and coat fully with the melted marshmallow mixture. Transfer the cereal mixture to the prepared dish, gently pressing it into an even layer. Let sit for 5 to 10 minutes.

4. Cut into 9 to 12 bars to serve. Store leftovers in an airtight container or zip-top bag at room temperature for up to 1 week.

Cooking tip: Use wet hands when pressing the cereal bars down to help keep them from sticking.

Make ahead tip: Wrap individual treats in plastic wrap and place in a freezer-safe container or zip-top bag. Freeze for up to 6 weeks. Thaw before serving.

CHEESECAKE SQUARES

MAKES 9 BARS | PREP TIME: 20 MINUTES, PLUS 2 HOURS TO CHILL | COOK TIME: 40 MINUTES
MAKE AHEAD | NUT-FREE

I love cheesecake more than I can say, but making an entire cheesecake can be tricky. These bars take the fuss out of cheesecake and deliver a no-fail treat every time. Easy to make, they are even easier to eat. I usually make these bars with a graham cracker crust, but I also love them with a vanilla wafer crust!

Nonstick baking spray

¾ cup finely crushed graham cracker crumbs

4 tablespoons (½ stick) unsalted butter, melted

¼ cup all-purpose flour

⅔ cup sugar, plus 2 tablespoons

12 ounces cream cheese, at room temperature

4 large eggs

1 tablespoon whole milk

1 teaspoon pure vanilla extract

1. Preheat the oven to 375°F. Mist a 9-inch square pan with baking spray. Set aside.

2. In a small bowl, using a fork, stir together the graham cracker crumbs, melted butter, flour, and 2 tablespoons of sugar until well mixed. Press the crust into the bottom of the prepared pan.

3. Bake for 8 minutes, or until lightly browned. Leave the oven on.

4. In a medium bowl, using a hand mixer, cream together the cream cheese and remaining ⅔ cup of sugar for 2 to 3 minutes, until combined and fluffy. Add the eggs, milk, and vanilla to the bowl and mix on low speed until fully incorporated. Pour the filling over the warm crust.

5. Bake for 30 minutes, or until the center looks set. Let cool to room temperature, then refrigerate for at least 2 hours and up to overnight. Cut into 9 bars to serve.

Addition tip: Top your cheesecake with fruit pie filling, jelly, or Homemade Caramel Sauce (page 155).

Make ahead tip: This recipe can be made ahead and refrigerated in an airtight container for up to 3 days before serving, or frozen for up to 3 months in an airtight container. Thaw before serving.

EASY APPLE CRISP

SERVES 4 TO 6 | PREP TIME: 15 MINUTES | COOK TIME: 45 MINUTES

5-INGREDIENT | NUT-FREE

This incredibly easy apple crisp is a fall staple. As it bakes, the apples soften and the sweet oat topping caramelizes. This dessert is especially good when served warm with a scoop of vanilla ice cream!

Nonstick baking spray

4 large green apples, cored, peeled, and sliced

¾ cup packed light brown sugar

½ cup rolled oats

½ cup all-purpose flour

8 tablespoons (1 stick) unsalted butter, melted

1. Preheat the oven to 350°F. Mist a square baking pan with baking spray.
2. Layer the apple slices across the bottom of the prepared pan.
3. In a medium bowl, stir together the brown sugar, oats, flour, and melted butter until well combined. Sprinkle the mixture over the apple slices.
4. Bake for 45 minutes, or until the apples are soft.
5. Refrigerate leftovers in an airtight container for up to 3 days.

Addition tip: Make this an Easy Apple Spice Crisp by stirring ½ teaspoon ground cinnamon and ⅛ teaspoon ground nutmeg into the oat mixture before sprinkling.

NO-CHURN VANILLA ICE CREAM

SERVES 6 | PREP TIME: 10 MINUTES, PLUS 4 HOURS TO FREEZE

5-INGREDIENT | GLUTEN-FREE | MAKE AHEAD | NUT-FREE

Did you know you can make smooth and creamy ice cream without an ice cream maker? This no-churn recipe base is a summer favorite in my house and you only need a handful of ingredients. Invest in a good-quality airtight container to extend the freezer life of your ice cream and avoid freezer burn.

1 (14-ounce) can sweetened condensed milk

1 tablespoon pure vanilla extract

2 cups heavy (whipping) cream

1. In a large bowl, stir together the sweetened condensed milk and vanilla to blend.

2. In a second large bowl, using a hand mixer, whip the heavy cream for about 5 minutes, until stiff peaks form. (If whipping by hand with a whisk, this process will take about 10 minutes.) Fold the whipped cream into the sweetened condensed milk mixture. Pour the batter into a freezer-safe container. Freeze for 4 hours, or until solid.

Ingredient tip: If you do not have pure vanilla extract, use the seeds of 1 vanilla bean or 1 teaspoon vanilla bean paste instead.

VARIATIONS

Chocolate: Add ½ cup cocoa powder to the sweetened condensed milk in step 1 and proceed as directed.

Cookies and Cream: Add 1½ cups crushed chocolate sandwich cookies to the sweetened condensed milk in step 1 and proceed as directed.

Lemon Crunch: Add ½ cup lemon curd plus 1 cup crushed vanilla wafer cookies to the sweetened condensed milk in step 1 and proceed as directed.

Strawberry: Add 2 cups diced fresh strawberries to the sweetened condensed milk in step 1 and proceed as directed.

CHOCOLATE SANDWICH COOKIE TRUFFLES

MAKES 24 TRUFFLES | PREP TIME: 30 MINUTES, PLUS 1 HOUR TO CHILL

5-INGREDIENT | NUT-FREE

Ready for another super-simple but delicious treat? Chocolate sandwich cookie truffles only have three ingredients, but they deliver unbeatable flavor! Swap the chocolate cookies for your favorite flavor, like vanilla or red velvet, for other fun flavor options.

18 chocolate sandwich cookies

4 ounces cream cheese, at room temperature

1 cup candy melts or chocolate chips

1. Line a sheet pan with parchment paper. Set aside.

2. In a high-powered blender or food processor, combine the cookies and cream cheese. Pulse until fully combined.

3. For each truffle, scoop about 2 tablespoons of dough and roll into a ball (you should get about 24 balls). Place on a plate and chill for 1 hour, or until firm.

4. Melt the candy melts according to the package directions.

5. Using a fork, one at a time, dip each chilled ball into the melted candy until fully covered and place it on the prepared sheet pan. Set on the countertop for about 20 minutes, or refrigerate for about 10 minutes, until the coating is set.

6. Refrigerate leftovers in an airtight container or zip-top bag for up to 2 weeks.

Addition tip: Add sprinkles or other decorations as desired.

Cooking tip: If you do not own a blender, place the cookies in a zip-top bag, seal it shut, and crush the cookies with a rolling pin until they are fine crumbs. Use a hand mixer to combine the crumbs with the cream cheese and proceed with step 3.

CHOCOLATE-PEANUT BUTTER CEREAL MIX

MAKES 4½ CUPS | PREP TIME: 15 MINUTES | COOK TIME: 2 MINUTES

5-INGREDIENT | 30-MINUTE | MAKE AHEAD

I've seen treats like these called Muddy Buddies and Puppy Chow—but by any name they are delicious. With only 5 ingredients and no baking required—these crunchy chocolate and peanut butter bites are a treat for the entire family.

4½ cups Rice Chex cereal

¾ cup powdered sugar

½ cup semisweet chocolate chips

¼ cup creamy peanut butter

2 tablespoons unsalted butter

1. Line a large sheet pan with aluminum foil. Set aside.

2. Place the cereal in a large bowl. Set aside. Place the powdered sugar in a large zip-top bag.

3. In a small microwave-safe dish, combine the chocolate chips, peanut butter, and butter. Heat on high power for 1 minute. Remove from the microwave and stir. Continue to heat in 20-second intervals, stirring after each, until melted. Pour the chocolate mixture over the cereal and toss well to coat.

4. Transfer the coated cereal to the bag with the powdered sugar. Seal the bag and gently shake until the cereal is well coated. Spread the mixture on the prepared sheet pan and let cool completely before serving.

Storage tip: Refrigerate in an airtight container for up to 2 weeks.

CONDIMENTS, SAUCES, DRESSINGS, AND SPICE MIXES

< Clockwise from top: Italian Dressing Seasoning, p. 157; Balsamic Vinaigrette, p. 147; Taco Seasoning, p. 156; Southern Barbecue Sauce, p. 149

HOMEMADE RANCH DRESSING

MAKES ABOUT 1½ CUPS (ABOUT 8 SERVINGS) | PREP TIME: 15 MINUTES, PLUS 1 HOUR TO CHILL

GLUTEN-FREE | MAKE AHEAD | NUT-FREE | ONE POT/PAN

This homemade ranch dressing is made with pantry-staple ingredients such as mayonnaise, sour cream, buttermilk, and dried seasonings. It's great served on any salad or as a dipping sauce for pizza.

½ cup mayonnaise

½ cup sour cream

½ cup buttermilk

½ teaspoon dried chives

½ teaspoon dried parsley

½ teaspoon dried dill weed

¼ teaspoon garlic powder

¼ teaspoon onion powder

Kosher salt

Freshly ground black pepper

1. In a blender, combine the mayonnaise, sour cream, buttermilk, chives, parsley, dill, garlic powder, onion power. Season with salt and pepper.

2. Puree for about 1 minute, until combined and smooth.

3. Transfer to a large lidded jar or airtight container. Refrigerate for at least 1 hour to thicken before serving. Keep leftovers refrigerated for up to 1 week.

Cooking tip: Use the freshest ingredients you can to increase the storage life of your dressing.

BALSAMIC VINAIGRETTE

MAKES ABOUT ¾ CUP (ABOUT 6 SERVINGS) | PREP TIME: 15 MINUTES

5-INGREDIENT | 30-MINUTE | DAIRY-FREE | GLUTEN-FREE | MAKE AHEAD | NUT-FREE |
ONE POT/PAN

I consider this an essential recipe because vinaigrette pairs well with almost every salad in this book. Plus, it tastes amazing on roasted vegetables or grilled chicken. Pick a quality balsamic vinegar, such as Napa Valley Naturals, as it contributes most of the flavor here.

½ cup extra-virgin olive oil

¼ cup balsamic vinegar

2 teaspoons light brown sugar

1½ teaspoons minced garlic

½ teaspoon kosher salt

½ teaspoon freshly ground black pepper

In a screw-top pint jar (such as a Mason jar), combine the oil, vinegar, brown sugar, garlic, salt, and pepper. Seal the lid and give the jar a good shake to combine the ingredients fully. Refrigerate for up to 2 weeks.

ITALIAN SALAD DRESSING

MAKES ABOUT 1 CUP (ABOUT 8 SERVINGS) | PREP TIME: 15 MINUTES

5-INGREDIENT | 30-MINUTE | DAIRY-FREE | GLUTEN-FREE | MAKE AHEAD | NUT-FREE |
ONE POT/PAN

This salad dressing is so quick to prepare, especially if you have my homemade Italian Dressing Seasoning (page 157) on hand! It is the perfect blend of spices, with just a hint of citrus. Make the dressing in advance and keep it refrigerated until you are ready to use it—it tastes better the longer it sits.

½ cup extra-virgin olive oil

¼ cup vinegar of choice

2 tablespoons water

1 tablespoon Italian Dressing Seasoning (page 157)

1 tablespoon freshly squeezed lemon juice

In a screw-top pint jar (such as a Mason jar), combine the oil, vinegar, water, Italian dressing seasoning, and lemon juice. Seal the lid and shake until combined. Refrigerate for up to 2 weeks.

Variation tip: Try different vinegar varieties, like balsamic vinegar, or red or white wine vinegar, for new flavor twists.

SOUTHERN BARBECUE SAUCE

**MAKES ABOUT 3 CUPS (ABOUT 12 SERVINGS) | PREP TIME: 10 MINUTES |
COOK TIME: 1 HOUR 10 MINUTES**

DAIRY-FREE | MAKE AHEAD | NUT-FREE | ONE POT/PAN

Wow everyone at your next grilling party with your very own homemade barbecue sauce!
It is as simple as adding all the ingredients to a pot and simmering to perfection. Try it on
my Go-To Grilled Chicken (page 72) or Easy Barbecue Pulled Pork (page 102).

2 cups ketchup

1 cup water

¼ cup loosely packed light
brown sugar

¼ cup granulated sugar

1 tablespoon freshly squeezed
lemon juice

1 tablespoon Worcestershire
sauce

1½ teaspoons freshly ground
black pepper

1½ teaspoons onion powder

1½ teaspoons dry mustard

1 teaspoon red pepper flakes

1 teaspoon garlic powder

1. In a medium saucepan, combine the ketchup,
   water, brown sugar, granulated sugar, lemon juice,
   Worcestershire sauce, black pepper, onion
   powder, mustard, red pepper flakes, and garlic
   powder. Bring to a boil over high heat. Reduce the
   heat to low and simmer for 1 hour, stirring frequently
   to prevent burning.

2. Cool slightly, then transfer to an airtight container and
   refrigerate for up to 2 weeks.

GARLIC BUTTER

MAKES 1 CUP (ABOUT 8 SERVINGS) | PREP TIME: 15 MINUTES

5-INGREDIENT | 30-MINUTE | GLUTEN-FREE | MAKE AHEAD | NUT-FREE | ONE POT/PAN

I always have garlic butter in my refrigerator. It works in so many recipes and can take flavors to the next level. Try it on Easy Baked Garlic Bread (page 118), melted over steak, for Garlic Butter Grilled Cheese (page 49), and even brushed onto pizza crust!

1 cup (2 sticks) salted butter, at room temperature

¼ cup grated Parmesan cheese

1 tablespoon minced garlic

2 teaspoons garlic powder

1 teaspoon Italian Seasoning (page 156) or store-bought seasoning

½ teaspoon freshly ground black pepper

In a medium bowl, combine the butter, Parmesan cheese, garlic, garlic powder, Italian seasoning, and pepper. Using a hand mixer, beat until combined and smooth. Refrigerate in an airtight container for up to 2 weeks.

GARLIC AND HERB PIZZA SAUCE

MAKES 1½ CUPS (ABOUT 6 SERVINGS) | PREP TIME: 15 MINUTES

30-MINUTE | GLUTEN-FREE | MAKE AHEAD | NUT-FREE

Making your own pizza sauce is easier than you think and makes homemade pizza shine. This recipe does not require any cooking, which means that in less than 15 minutes you can spread tomato goodness onto your prepared crust or have a delicious dipping sauce.

1 (6-ounce) can tomato paste

¾ cup water

2 tablespoons grated Parmesan cheese

1 tablespoon sugar

1 teaspoon garlic powder

¾ teaspoon onion powder

¼ teaspoon kosher salt

¼ teaspoon dried basil

¼ teaspoon dried oregano

¼ teaspoon dried parsley

¼ teaspoon red pepper flakes

1. In a medium bowl, stir together the tomato paste and water, adding the latter a little at a time, until blended and the sauce reaches your desired thickness.
2. Add the Parmesan cheese, sugar, garlic powder, onion powder, salt, basil, oregano, parsley, and red pepper flakes. Whisk to combine.
3. Use immediately, refrigerate in an airtight container for up to 5 days, or freeze for up to 2 months.

FRY SAUCE

MAKES ABOUT ½ CUP (ABOUT 4 SERVINGS) | PREP TIME: 10 MINUTES

5-INGREDIENT | 30-MINUTE | DAIRY-FREE | GLUTEN-FREE | MAKE AHEAD | NUT-FREE | ONE POT/PAN

Fry sauce is big in Utah. Each restaurant has its own version, and all are insanely good. The magic starts with a mixture of mayonnaise and ketchup. Use it on French fries, Juicy Homemade Burgers (page 107), or as a different topping on hot dogs.

¼ cup mayonnaise

2 tablespoons ketchup

1 tablespoon sweet pickle relish

¾ teaspoon sugar

¾ teaspoon distilled white vinegar

In a small bowl, stir together the mayonnaise, ketchup, relish, sugar, and vinegar until well combined. Serve immediately or refrigerate in an airtight container for up to 2 weeks.

HONEY MUSTARD DIPPING SAUCE

MAKES ABOUT 1 CUP (ABOUT 8 SERVINGS) | PREP TIME: 10 MINUTES

5-INGREDIENT | 30-MINUTE | DAIRY-FREE | GLUTEN-FREE | MAKE AHEAD | NUT-FREE |
ONE POT/PAN

This recipe was originally created for my Crispy Dijon Baked Chicken (page 73), but has turned into a must-have for any chicken dish—and for grilled cheese! The secret is using two types of mustard and just a touch of honey. You get that spicy tang with a little sweetness.

½ cup plus 1 tablespoon
mayonnaise

6 tablespoons Dijon mustard

1 tablespoon prepared
yellow mustard

1 tablespoon honey

In a small bowl, stir together the mayonnaise, Dijon mustard, yellow mustard, and honey until blended. Serve immediately or refrigerate in an airtight container for up to 2 weeks.

STRAWBERRY SAUCE

MAKES 1½ CUPS (ABOUT 6 SERVINGS) | PREP TIME: 10 MINUTES | COOK TIME: 20 MINUTES

5-INGREDIENT | 30-MINUTE | DAIRY-FREE | GLUTEN-FREE | MAKE AHEAD | NUT-FREE |
ONE POT/PAN

This sauce is ideal for biscuits, ice cream, pancakes, or waffles. Fresh berries, sugar, and vanilla are simmered to create a sauce that is welcome at any brunch.

1 pint strawberries, washed, hulled, and roughly chopped

⅓ cup sugar

1 teaspoon pure vanilla extract

1. In a large pot, combine the strawberries, sugar, and vanilla. Bring the mixture to a simmer and cook for 15 minutes.

2. Serve immediately, or let the sauce cool, then transfer to an airtight container and refrigerate for up to 4 days.

Variation tip: Substitute blueberries for the strawberries and stir in ¼ teaspoon almond extract for a sweet variation.

HOMEMADE CARAMEL SAUCE

MAKES 1½ CUPS (ABOUT 12 SERVINGS) | PREP TIME: 5 MINUTES | COOK TIME: 10 MINUTES
5-INGREDIENT | 30-MINUTE | GLUTEN-FREE | MAKE AHEAD | NUT-FREE | ONE POT/PAN

Do not let homemade caramel intimidate you. This recipe takes less than 15 minutes to make and is a decadent topping for Cheesecake Squares (page 138), No-Churn Vanilla Ice Cream (page 140), or Crisp and Fluffy Waffles (page 13)! The secret is cooking over low heat and stirring constantly to avoid burning.

1 cup packed light brown sugar

½ cup half-and-half

4 tablespoons (½ stick) unsalted butter

1 tablespoon pure vanilla extract

1½ teaspoons fleur de sel (optional)

1. In a medium saucepan over medium-low heat, combine the brown sugar, half-and-half, and butter. Cook for 5 to 6 minutes, whisking constantly, until the sauce thickens slightly. Stir in the vanilla and fleur de sel (if using).

2. Remove from the heat and let the caramel cool slightly before serving.

3. Refrigerate leftovers in an airtight container or jar for up to 2 weeks.

Ingredient tip: If you do not have half-and-half, use heavy (whipping) cream. Fleur de sel is a finishing salt. You can find it online and in most gourmet grocery stores.

QUICK AND EASY SPICE SEASONINGS

YIELDS VARY | PREP TIME: 10 MINUTES

30-MINUTE | DAIRY-FREE | GLUTEN-FREE | MAKE AHEAD | NUT-FREE | ONE POT/PAN

Occasionally you find yourself in need of a seasoning mix, like the taco seasoning called for in my Beef Taco Salad (page 42) or Italian seasoning for my Italian Sausage Lasagna Soup (page 31). You can make your own seasoning blends with spices you probably have in your pantry. The following recipes are for the homemade spice mixes I use in my recipes in place of store-bought varieties. Homemade means you get to control exactly what goes in them and start with the freshest ingredients for the best flavors.

To make all seasoning variations: In an airtight container with a lid (such as a Mason jar), combine all the ingredients. Seal the lid and shake until combined. Store in the container in a cool, dry place for up to 1 year until ready to use.

ITALIAN SEASONING

MAKES ABOUT ¾ CUP

2 tablespoons dried basil

2 tablespoons dried cilantro or ground coriander

2 tablespoons dried marjoram

2 tablespoons dried oregano

2 tablespoons dried rosemary

2 tablespoons dried thyme

1½ teaspoons red pepper flakes

TACO SEASONING

MAKES ABOUT ¾ CUP

Use about 2 tablespoons per every 1 pound of meat in the recipe.

6 tablespoons chili powder

2 tablespoons ground cumin

2 tablespoons kosher salt

2 tablespoons freshly ground black pepper

1 tablespoon paprika

1½ teaspoons garlic powder

1½ teaspoons onion powder

1½ teaspoons dried oregano

¾ teaspoon cayenne pepper

FAJITA SEASONING

MAKES ABOUT ¼ CUP

Use about 2 tablespoons per every 1 pound of meat in the recipe.

1 tablespoon ground cumin

1 tablespoon kosher salt

1½ teaspoons dried oregano

1½ teaspoons chili powder

1½ teaspoons paprika

SALAD SPRINKLE

MAKES ABOUT ¼ CUP

This is delicious sprinkled on green salads, pasta salads, chicken, and vegetables, and on top of homemade breads to season them before baking.

4½ teaspoons sesame seeds

1 tablespoon paprika

2¼ teaspoons kosher salt

1½ teaspoons celery seed

¾ teaspoon garlic powder

¾ teaspoon freshly ground black pepper

¼ teaspoon cayenne pepper

ITALIAN DRESSING SEASONING

MAKES ABOUT ¼ CUP

See Italian Salad Dressing (page 148) for a simple vinaigrette idea using this seasoning.

1 tablespoon dried oregano

1½ teaspoons kosher salt

1½ teaspoons garlic salt

1½ teaspoons onion powder

1½ teaspoons sugar

1½ teaspoons dried parsley

½ teaspoon freshly ground black pepper

½ teaspoon dried basil

⅛ teaspoon dried thyme

⅛ teaspoon celery salt

HAMBURGER SEASONING

MAKES SCANT ¼ CUP

For tasty burgers or meatloaf, use 1 tablespoon seasoning per every 1 pound of meat in the recipe.

3¾ teaspoons paprika

2¼ teaspoons kosher salt

1½ teaspoons freshly ground black pepper

¾ teaspoon light brown sugar

¾ teaspoon garlic powder

¾ teaspoon onion powder

POT ROAST SEASONING

MAKES ABOUT 1 CUP

Use 2 tablespoons seasoning for every 1 pound of meat in the recipe.

6 tablespoons light brown sugar

3 tablespoons garlic powder

2 tablespoons onion powder

2 tablespoons kosher salt

1 tablespoon dried oregano

1 tablespoon dried thyme

1 tablespoon dried parsley

1 tablespoon freshly ground black pepper

ONION SOUP MIX

MAKES ABOUT ¼ CUP

Mix 2 tablespoons soup mix with 16 ounces sour cream for a fantastic chip and veggie dip. Sprinkle the dry mix on meat, vegetables, or anything else that would be improved by a bit of onion zing.

4 beef bouillon cubes, crushed

2½ tablespoons dried minced onion

1 teaspoon onion powder

⅛ teaspoon freshly ground black pepper

HOMEMADE BREAD CRUMBS

MAKES 1½ CUPS | PREP TIME: 5 MINUTES | COOK TIME: 40 MINUTES

5-INGREDIENT | DAIRY-FREE | MAKE AHEAD | NUT-FREE | ONE POT/PAN

Making your own bread crumbs is easy and a great way to use day-old bread. Keep these bread crumbs on hand as an easy add-in to meatloaf, to top macaroni and cheese, or to sprinkle on soup for a bit of texture!

10 bread slices

1. Preheat the oven to 250°F.
2. Place the bread in a single layer on a large sheet pan. Bake for 20 minutes per side.
3. Remove from the oven and let cool completely.
4. Place the toasted bread into a high-powered blender or food processor. Pulse for 1 to 2 minutes, or until the bread is a fine crumb. Transfer the bread crumbs to an airtight container or zip-top bag and keep at room temperature for up to 1 month.

Ingredient tip: Any day-old bread will work for this recipe, but thick-cut French bread works especially well.

Variation tip: To make Italian-style bread crumbs, follow the instructions for Homemade Bread Crumbs and stir in 1 tablespoon Italian Seasoning (page 156) or store-bought Italian seasoning before storing.

MEASUREMENT CONVERSIONS

VOLUME EQUIVALENTS (LIQUID)

US STANDARD	US STANDARD (OUNCES)	METRIC (APPROXIMATE)
2 tablespoons	1 fl. oz.	30 mL
¼ cup	2 fl. oz.	60 mL
½ cup	4 fl. oz.	120 mL
1 cup	8 fl. oz.	240 mL
1½ cups	12 fl. oz.	355 mL
2 cups or 1 pint	16 fl. oz.	475 mL
4 cups or 1 quart	32 fl. oz.	1 L
1 gallon	128 fl. oz.	4 L

VOLUME EQUIVALENTS (DRY)

US STANDARD	METRIC (APPROXIMATE)
⅛ teaspoon	0.5 mL
¼ teaspoon	1 mL
½ teaspoon	2 mL
¾ teaspoon	4 mL
1 teaspoon	5 mL
1 tablespoon	15 mL
¼ cup	59 mL
⅓ cup	79 mL
½ cup	118 mL
⅔ cup	156 mL
¾ cup	177 mL
1 cup	235 mL
2 cups or 1 pint	475 mL
3 cups	700 mL
4 cups or 1 quart	1 L

OVEN TEMPERATURES

FAHRENHEIT	CELSIUS (APPROXIMATE)
250°F	120°C
300°F	150°C
325°F	165°C
350°F	180°C
375°F	190°C
400°F	200°C
425°F	220°C
450°F	230°C

WEIGHT EQUIVALENTS

US STANDARD	METRIC (APPROXIMATE)
½ ounce	15 g
1 ounce	30 g
2 ounces	60 g
4 ounces	115 g
8 ounces	225 g
12 ounces	340 g
16 ounces or 1 pound	455 g

< Chicken and Mushroom Thai-Style Coconut Soup, p. 34

RECIPE INDEX

5-INGREDIENT

30-MINUTE

MAKE AHEAD

ONE POT/PAN

SLOW COOKER

INDEX

ACKNOWLEDGMENTS

To my son, Dax. Thank you for being my ultimate taste tester and for making my recipes. You are my star helper, and your input was appreciated more than you will ever know. Thank you to the friends and family who tirelessly made these recipes and sent valuable feedback! It is because of you that I was able to add so many tasty dishes to this book! To my readers, thank you for making and sharing my recipes. The love and support I get from each of you has filled me with passion and helped inspire each new recipe.

ABOUT THE AUTHOR

 **Jesseca Hallows** is the recipe developer and photographer behind the website *One Sweet Appetite* and the author of *The Deliciously Easy Cupcake Cookbook*. Her passion for food has driven her to create beautiful and tasty recipes the entire family will enjoy. Visit OneSweetAppetite.com for more great recipes, and follow Jesseca on Instagram @1SweetAppetite.

CPSIA information can be obtained
at www.ICGtesting.com
Printed in the USA
JSHW030503170920
8003JS00005B/16

9 781647 398712